Introduction to Gnosis

THE BUDDHA MAITREYA

There is Gnosis in the Buddhist doctrine, in the Tantric
Buddhism from Tibet, in the Zen Buddhism from Japan,
in the Chan Buddhism of China, in Sufism, in the Whirling
Dervishes, in the Egyptian, Persian, Chaldean, Pythagorean,
Greek, Aztec, Mayan, Inca, etc., wisdom.

Introduction to
Gnosis

Practical Steps to Awaken the Consciousness

Samael Aun Weor

Thelema Press
2007

Our life is shaped by our mind;
We become what we think.
- The Buddha Shakyamuni

You are what you are because of the mind.
- Samael Aun Weor

Introduction to Gnosis
A Thelema Press Book/February 2007
English Edition © 2007 Thelema Press

ISBN 978-1-934206-08-9

Thelema Press is a non-profit organization delivering to humanity the teachings of
Samael Aun Weor. All proceeds go to further the distribution of these books. For
more information, visit our website.

www.gnosticteachings.org
www.gnosticradio.org
www.gnosticschool.org
www.gnosticstore.org
www.gnosticvideos.org

Contents

First Degree of Introduction to Gnosis 1
Lesson One 3
   An Exercise to Control Your Anger 5
Lesson Two 7
   The Power of Thought 7
   Mental Force 9
   Concentration of the Mind 9
   The Law of Karma 10
   Favorable Circumstances 10
   Exercise 11
The Descent of Cosmic Vibration 12
Lesson Three 13
   Prana 14
   The Names of the Tattvas 14
   Tattwic Timetable 15
   Properties of the Tattvas 15
   Akash 15
   Vayu 15
   Tejas 16
   Prithvi 16
   Apas 16
   Exercise 17
Lesson Four 19
   Exercise 20
   Exercise 21
Lesson Five 23
   Money 23
   Exercise 26
Lesson Six 27
   Exercise Before the Mirror 29
   Clairvoyance 30
Lesson Seven 31
   Exercise 34
Lesson Eight 35
   Alcoholism 35
   Initiation 35
   Intoxication 36
   Death 36
   Psychology of the Drunkard 37
   Campaign Against Alcohol 37

The Home - True Education Begins at Home 37
Meditation and Intoxication 38
Alcoholic Larvae...38
Osmotherapy 39
Treatment 39
Exercise...39
Mental Relaxation 40
Concentration 40
Meditation...40
Contemplation 41
Lesson Nine 43
The Universal Mind...43
Imagination and Will...44
Mental Action...44
Mental Epidemics..44
Mental Hygiene 45
Origins of the Universal Mind..45
Terms 46
Exercise...47
Appendix 49
Vegetarian Diet...49
How to Make the Light Within Ourselves 51
Self-observation 54
Chatter...57
"I's" in the Five Centers 59
Matrimony, Divorce and Tantrism 63
Tantrism...71
Index...79

First Degree of Introduction to Gnosis

This is the introductory degree to the **Gnostic** philosophical studies or **External** degrees of Gnosis. It is natural that all students will begin with this degree and eventually continue with the first, second, third degrees, etc. One should keep in mind that these are not the esoteric Gnostic degrees. The esoteric Gnostic degrees, which are the authentic ones, cannot be revealed by anyone who has received them; this is forbidden. Whoever says: "I have so many degrees, so many Initiations," is being dishonest.

If a person wants to become an engineer, lawyer, doctor, etc. he has to prepare himself for it. That person will go to school and study a great deal. After he has a good theoretical basis in the field he studied, he will begin to practice what he has learned. Practice brings about perfection. The great sages, professionals, scientists, etc. have not merely had a theoretical knowledge of their respective fields of study, but have also put this knowledge to practice. Theory by itself cannot bring about anything except an intellectual enjoyment on the part of those who understand it.

Study these lessons and study them with true incentive, with the desire to learn, with the desire of understanding the superior knowledge. But remember that you need to put into practice what you learn if you want to achieve the perfection of the work.

Gnosis: from the Greek *gnosis*, "knowledge," "to know." This term is traditionally used in to indicate experiential, direct knowledge, or the knowledge gained through intimate personal experience.

Lesson One

It is necessary to be successful in life. If you want to be successful, you should begin by being sincere with yourself; recognize your own errors. When we recognize our errors we are on the path to correcting them. Everyone who corrects his own errors is inevitably successful. The businessman who daily blames others for his own failures and never recognizes his own errors will not be successful. Remember that the greatest criminals consider themselves to be saints. If we visit a penitentiary we will prove to ourselves that none of the criminals consider themselves guilty. Almost all of them say to themselves, "I am innocent." Don't make the same mistake, have the courage to recognize your own errors. Thus will you escape greater evils.

Whoever recognizes his own errors can make a happy home. The politician, scientist, philosopher, and the religious person, etc. that comes to recognize his mistakes can correct them and be successful in life.

If you want to triumph in life, don't criticize anyone. Whoever criticizes another person is a weakling. And the one who criticizes himself every moment is a giant. Criticism is useless because it hurts the pride of others and provokes the resistance of the victim who then seeks to justify himself. Criticism provokes an inevitable reaction against its maker. If you want to truly triumph in life, listen to this advice. Do not criticize anyone.

The man or woman who knows how to live without criticizing anyone does not provoke resistance nor reactions on the part of his fellowmen, and consequently creates an atmosphere of success and progress. On the other hand, he who criticizes others has many enemies. We have to remember that human beings are full of pride and vanity, and this vanity inherent in them produces a reaction (resentment, hate, etc.) that is directed towards the one who criticizes them. He who wants to correct others should best begin by correcting himself. This gives better results and is less dangerous.

The world is full of neurasthenic persons.† The neurasthenic type is a faultfinder, irritable, and intolerable. There are many causes of neurasthenia: impatience, anger, egotism, arrogance, etc.

A mediator exists between the Spirit and the body: the nervous system. Take care of your nervous system. When your nervous system is irritated by something that exhausts you, it is better to flee from it. Work intensely but with moderation. Remember that excessive work produces fatigue. If you do not pay attention to fatigue, if you continue with excessive work, then fatigue is replaced with excitement. When excitement turns morbid, it becomes neurasthenia. It is necessary to alternate work with pleasant rest so as to avoid the danger of falling into neurasthenia.

Every employer who wants to succeed should be careful of not falling into neurasthenia. The neurasthenic employer criticizes everything and becomes unbearable. The neurasthenic despises patience and as employer becomes the executioner of his employees. Workers who must work under the orders of a neurasthenic and faultfinding employer end up hating the job and the employer. No discontented worker works with pleasure. Many times enterprises fail because the workers are discontented, dissatisfied and do not work efficiently in such circumstances.

The neurasthenic, as worker or office employee, becomes rebellious and ends up being fired from his job.

Every neurasthenic worker seeks any occasion to criticize his employer. Every employer has pride and vanity and it is obvious that he feels offended when his employees criticize him. The worker who lives criticizing his employer ends up losing his job.

Take care of your nervous system. Work moderately. Enjoy yourself healthily. Do not criticize anyone. Try to see the best in all human beings.

---

† Neurasthenia: A category of mental disorder that is no longer in use. It described a condition with symptoms such as irritability, fatigue, weakness, anxiety, and localized pains without any apparant physical causes. It was thought to result from exhaustion of the nervous system.

An Exercise to Control Your Anger

Do you feel irritated or full of anger? Are you nervous? Reflect a little: remember that anger can provoke gastric ulcers. Control anger through breathing: inhale the vital air very slowly (do not inhale through your mouth; inhale through your nose, keeping your mouth properly closed), mentally counting 1-2-3-4-5-6. Hold the breath mentally counting 1-2-3-4-5-6. Now exhale the breath very slowly through your mouth, mentally counting 1-2-3-4-5-6. Repeat the exercise until your anger subsides.

May peace be with you!

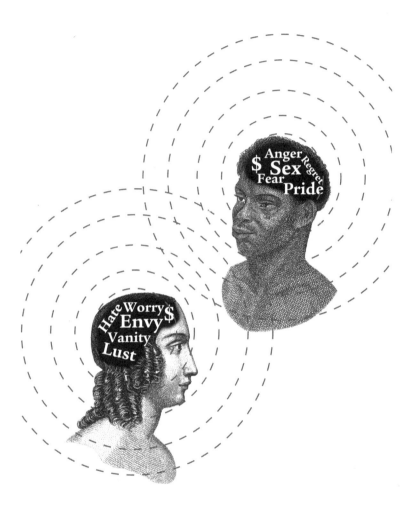

We have had thousands and thousands of wars and we are everlastingly talking about peace; but the way we live our daily lives is a war, a battlefield, a conflict... We have never asked ourselves whether we can live a life of complete peace, which means without conflict of any kind. Conflict exists because there is contradiction in ourselves.

- J. Krishnamurti

Lesson Two

A great author deduced that the human being needs eight important things in life: health and the conservation of life, nourishment, sleep, money and the things money can buy, life in the beyond, sexual satisfaction, the well-being of his children and a sense of proper importance. We synthesize these eight things into three:

1. Health
2. Money
3. Love

If your really want to acquire these three things, you should study and practice everything that this course teaches you. We will show you the path of success.

The Power of Thought

It is necessary for you to know that an immensely superior power greater than electricity and dynamite exists: that is, the power of mind. When you think of a friend or a member of the family, etc., mental waves escape from your brain. These waves are similar to those of a radio transmitter. These waves travel through space and reach the mind of the person you are thinking about. Scientists have already began to experiment with the power of the mind. Soon, the telementometer will be invented (an instrument with which the mental forces of each person will be measured). In the future, optics will advance some more and then the photomentometer will be invented (an instrument that will allow us to see and measure the mental force that is radiated by the human brain).

You must know that just as man has a mind, the entire universe also has a mind. The human mind and the cosmic mind exist. The earth is condensed mind. The entire Universe is condensed mind. Universal Mind waves saturate the infinite space.

The first thing that an architect who will build a house does is to create the project mentally. He constructs it in his mind, projects it on the plan and lastly crystallizes it materially. Thus, everything, every building first existed in the mind. Nothing can exist in the physical or material world in which we live before having existed in the World of the Mind.

It is necessary to learn how to concentrate and project the mind with precision and great force. It is necessary for you to know that to concentrate the mind is to fix your attention on a single object. When you fix your attention on a distant friend, when you concentrate on that friend, you can be certain that your brain emits powerful mental waves that will inevitably reach your friend's brain. What is important is for you to truly concentrate. It is necessary that no other thought be capable of distracting you. You should learn how to concentrate your mind.

You are studying this course and we believe that you want to succeed in life and have health, money and love. Reflect a little: learn how to use mental power. Whoever learns how to use the power of thought proceeds to success with absolute certainty as the arrow guided by the hand of the expert archer reaches its target. Remember that the world is a product of the mind. You are what you are because of the mind. You can totally change yourself by using mental power. The poor and miserable are like that because they want to be so; they keep themselves miserable and poor with their mind. The rich and powerful person is so because he made himself that way with his mind. Each person is what he wants to be with the power of the mind. Each person projects into the World of Cosmic Mind what he is and what he wants to be. The projects of the mind physically crystallize and we then have in the physical world our rich or miserable, happy or disgraceful life.

Everything depends on the type of mental projections that have crystallized. As the cloud condenses into water and the water freezes into ice, so does mental energy: first, clouds (projects), then water (circumstances, development of the project), and lastly, hard ice (the project converted into concrete facts or things). If the project has been well done and with enough strength, if the actions or the development of the facts and circumstances have been marvelous, victory will be the result. The perfect condensation of a project is victory.

The basic factors for the success of a project are three:
1. Mental Force
2. Favorable Circumstances
3. Intelligence

Mental Force

Without mental force it is impossible to achieve the crystallization of a project (commercial, etc.). It is necessary for our students to learn how to use mental force. But it is necessary for the student to first learn how to relax his physical body. It is indispensable to know how to relax the body to achieve the perfect concentration of the mind. We can relax the body seated in a comfortable chair or lying down in the corpse posture (with our heels touching each other, arms close to our sides, etc.). The second of the two positions (the corpse posture) is the better.

Imagine that your feet are subtle, that a group of dwarves escape from them. Imagine that your calves are full of small playful dwarves that leave one by one and that as they leave, the muscles become flexible and elastic. Continue with your knees performing the same exercise. Continue with the thighs, sexual organs, abdomen, heart, throat, face and head muscles successively, imagining that those small dwarves flee from each of those parts of the body, leaving the muscles completely relaxed.

Concentration of the Mind

When the body is perfectly relaxed, mental concentration becomes easy and simple. Concentrate on the business you have in mind. Vividly imagine the entire business, the people that are related to the work. Identify yourself with those people. Speak as if you were them; mentally say what you would like those people to say. Forget about yourself and change your human personality to that of those persons, acting the way you would like them to act. Thus you will define powerful thought waves that will go through space and reach the brains of the persons related with the business. If the concentration is perfect, success will then be inevitable.

The Law of Karma

This law is well known in the Orient. Millions of people in the entire world know of it because this Law is Universal. This law operates in the whole Universe. If you misuse the power of the mind, the Law of Karma will fall upon you and you will be horribly punished.

Mental energy is a gift of God and should only be utilized for good purposes and with good intentions. It is just for the poor to better their economic situation, but it is not just to utilize mental power to harm people. Before doing a mental exercise to carry out the crystallization of a project, reflect and meditate: if you will use mental power to harm others, it is better not to do it because the terrible Ray of Cosmic Justice will inevitably fall upon you like a ray of vengeance.

Favorable Circumstances

Thought and action should always march totally united. Materialization is only possible when the circumstances are favorable. Learn how to determine favorable circumstances for your business. Freud, the great psychologist, said that everything that man does in life has two fundamental causes: (1) sexual impulse, (2) the desire to be great. Every human being is motivated by the sexual impulse. Everybody wants to be appreciated. Nobody likes to be despised. If you want to be surrounded by good circumstances for the crystallization of your business, then recognize the good qualities of your fellowmen; do not humiliate anyone. Do not despise anyone. It is necessary to encourage each individual in his job, office or profession. By means of appreciation and encouragement, we can awaken enthusiasm in all those people that relate to us. Learn how to wisely praise your fellowmen without failing into flattery. People feel reassured with the food of esteem. Be gentlemanly; do not criticize anyone, thus you will form a favorable atmosphere for the crystallization of your business. The sincere appreciation of the merits of one's fellowman is one of the great secrets of success.

It is necessary to abandon the bad habit of talking about ourselves at every moment. It is urgent to employ the Verb to strengthen and encourage the good qualities of our fellowman. The Gnostic student should abandon the extremely bad habit of naming himself and telling the story of his life at every moment. The man or woman who only talks of himself or herself becomes unbearable. Persons like this fall into misery because people become tired of them.

Never say, "I." Always say, "We." The term "We" has more cosmic power. The term "I" is egotistical and tires all those who come in contact with us. The "I" is egotistical. The "I" should be dissolved. The "I" is a creator of conflicts and problems. Always repeat: "we, we, we,..."

Every morning before getting out of bed, say with force and energy: "We are strong. We are rich. We are filled with luck and harmony; Om, Om, Om." Recite this simple prayer and you will see that you are prosperous in everything. Have great devotion in this prayer. Have faith.

Exercise

Hang a silk thread from the ceiling of your room. A needle should be at the end of the thread.

Concentrate on that needle and try to move it with the power of your mind.

When developed, mental waves can move this needle. Work ten minutes daily on this exercise. In the beginning, the needle at the end of the silk thread will not move. With time, you will see that the needle oscillates and moves vigorously. This exercise is to develop mental power. Remember that mental waves travel through space and pass from one brain to the next.

May peace be with you!

The Descent of Cosmic Vibration

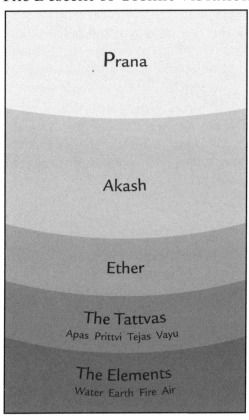

Prana

Akash

Ether

The Tattvas
Apas Prittvi Tejas Vayu

The Elements
Water Earth Fire Air

Lesson Three

The great lawyer Jose M. Seseras said the following:

"There is no luck or misfortune, success or failure; everything is a vibration of the ether."

By learning the use of the Tattvas one can favorably solve all matters in life.

You need a precise and exact system to obtain money; a scientific system that never falls. You need to take advantage of favorable circumstances to achieve the crystallization of all your projects (commercial, etc.).

Remember: a Tattva is a vibration of the ether. In this age of radio, television and teleguided missiles, it is absurd to deny the vibration of the ether. A great sage said:

"Life was born from radiation, subsists because of radiation and is suppressed by any oscillatory imbalance."

You have the right to succeed. Spirit should overcome matter. We cannot accept misery. Remember that misery is a property of failed souls. When the Spirit overcomes matter, the result is Light, splendor, complete success economically, socially, and spiritually.

It Is necessary that you learn the Law of Universal Vibration. The study of the Tattvas is very important. A Tattva (this is a Hindustani term) is a vibration of the ether. Now scientists say that the ether does not exist and that the only thing that really exists is the magnetic field. We could also say that matter does not exist and that energy is the only thing that is real. These are words, a matter of terms. The magnetic field is the ether.

"All comes from ether; everything returns to ether."

Sir Oliver Lodge, the great British scientist, said, "It is the ether that gives place, through diverse modifications of its equilibrium, to all phenomena of the Universe, from the impalpable Light to the formidable masses of the worlds."

Prana

Prana is the cosmic energy. Prana is vibration, electric motion, light and heat, universal magnetism, life. Prana is the life that throbs in each atom and in each sun. Prana is the life of ether. The Great Life, in other words, Prana, is transformed into a very divine, intensely blue substance. The name of this substance is **Akash**. The Akash is a marvelous substance that fills the entire infinite space and when it is modified it becomes ether. It is very interesting to know that the ether, when modified, becomes what we call the Tattvas.

The study of the vibrations of the ether (Tattvas) is indispensable. Remember that business, love, health. etc. are controlled by cosmic vibrations. If you know the vibratory laws of life, if you know the Tattvas, you will be able to obtain much money. Remember that money in itself is not good or bad; everything depends on its use. It is good if you use it for good, evil if you use it for evil. Obtain much money and use it for the good of humanity.

There are seven Tattvas that you should learn to use to succeed in life. No Gnostic student should live in misery. It is necessary that you know the names of the seven Tattvas. These names are Sanskrit terms. It is possible that it might be somewhat difficult to learn these names but remember that studying is well worth it to succeed in life.

The Names of the Tattvas

Akash is the principle of ether.

Vayu is the etheric principle of the air.

Tejas is the etheric principle of fire.

Prithvi is the etheric principle of the element earth.

Apas is the etheric principle of water.

There are two secret Tattvas named **Adi** and **Samadhi** that vibrate during the Aurora (dawn) and are excellent for internal meditation (Ecstasy or Samadhi is achieved with them). We will not expand on these Tattvas now because they are useful to advanced students only.

Tattwic Timetable*

The vibration of the Tattvas begins at sunrise. Each Tattva vibrates for twenty-four minutes in a period of two hours. The first Tattva that vibrates is Akash, followed in succession by Vayu, Tejas, Prithvi, and Apas. Two hours later, Akash vibrates again and the succession of Tattvas in the same order is repeated. The Tattvas vibrate day and night.

It is necessary to know the hour of sunrise. Bucheli's *Astrological Yearbook* is one of the calendars that marks the time of sunrise in each country of Latin America. Some daily newspapers (especially in the United States of America) and magazines indicate the time of sunrise. *Galvan's Calendar* is also good for this purpose. Those who would like Bucheli's *American Yearbook* (in Spanish) can request it from the following address: Mrs. Elly de Buchelli, Casilla 1880, Santiago de Chile, S.A.

* Editor's Note: Samael Aun Weor wrote this section based upon the investigations of other occultists. Upon further investigation of his own, he later wrote that such timetables are discordant, and that "the best Tattwic day-timer is the one from Nature." (*Occult Medicine and Practical Magic*, pgs 28-29, Thelema Press edition).

Properties of the Tattvas

Akash

Akash is exclusively good for meditation. We advise you to pray a lot during this time. Do not have business or love appointments during this time because you will inevitably fail. This Tattva causes us to make very serious mistakes. If you work during this period, you should then be very careful. (Artists should abstain from working in Akash). Everything that begins with Akash will fail. Akash is the Tattva of death.

Vayu

Everything that is velocity and motion corresponds to Vayu, the principle of air. Winds, air, aerial navigation, etc. are related to Vayu. During this period people enjoy speaking ill about their fellowmen, lying, stealing, etc. Usually, airplane accidents happen during this period. Suicides are stimulated by this Tattva. We advise you not to marry during this period because your marriage will be of a short duration. All kinds of simple and fast businesses are very good in Vayu, but businesses that are complex and of long duration result in failure. It is good to carry out intellectual works during this period. The great yogis mentally manipulate this Tattva and use it intelligently when they want to float in the air.

Tejas

Tejas is hot because it is the etheric principle of fire. During the period in which this Tattva is active we feel more heat. You can bathe in cold water in Tejas and you will never catch a cold. Never argue with anyone in Tejas because the consequences can be serious. You should utilize the time of Tejas to work intensely. Do not marry during Tejas because you will have constant quarrels with your partner. The most terrible explosions and accidents happen in the period of the Tattva Tejas.

Prithvi

This is the Tattva of success in life. If you want to succeed in business, do it in Prithvi. If you want to have good health, eat and drink in Prithvi. Marriages accomplished in Prithvi are happy for life. Every party, lecture, business or appointment done in Prithvi will be a total success. Prithvi is love, charity, benevolence.

Apas

Apas is the principle of water and is the opposite of Tejas (fire). This Tattva is marvellous for the purchase of merchandise. It is marvellous for business and you will be able to earn much money if you know how to take advantage of this Tattva. Buy lottery tickets in Apas; journeys by water are good in Apas. Rainfalls that begin in Apas tend to be very lengthy and heavy. The Tattva Apas works in concentrating and attracting.

Remember that you need to know the exact time of sunrise to be guided by the Tattvas. Always have a good wristwatch or pocket watch and take advantage of the Tattvas in practical life.

Exercise

Sit at a table facing the Orient, rest your elbows on the table and proceed in the following manner:

Introduce the thumbs of your right and left hands into your ears. Cover your eyes with the index fingers, cover your nostrils with your middle fingers, and seal your lips with your ring fingers and little fingers.

Inhale slowly counting from one to twenty. Exhale slowly counting one to twenty. It is necessary to remove your middle fingers to inhale and exhale. But during the retention of your breath, the middle fingers should hermetically seal your nostrils. It is necessary for you to try to see the Tattvas with the Third Eye durind the retention of your breath. The Third Eye resides between the two eyebrows. At the beginning you will see nothing, but after some time you will be able to see and recognize them by their colors. Akash is black and its planet is Saturn. Vayu is greenish-blue and Mercury is its planet. Tejas is red as fire and its planet is Mars. Prithvi is golden yellow and the Sun is its planet; it is also influenced by Jupiter. Apas is white and Venus and the Moon are its planets.

May peace be with you!

"Follow me, and I will make you fishers of men."
- Mark 1:16

Lesson Four

In order to succeed in life one has to become a fisher of men. Jesus chose his disciples amongst poor fishermen. They had to stop catching fish to become fishers of men. Do you want to obtain success, power, glory? Listen to this advice: "Put bait on the hook that will catch the fish."

Do not talk with others about things of interest to you. Your business is your business. Unfortunately, the human being is egotistical and only wants to know things of his interest. If you talk to your fellowman about the things he desires and loves, you will influence him positively and will obtain from him all that you need.

We need to learn to see the other person's point of view and help to solve his conflicts; in this manner we solve our own problems. Become an altruistic and generous person. Help others with your advice; do your best to understand the point of view of others and you will fish in abundance. When we begin comprehending our fellowmen, we also begin to take the first steps on the path of happiness and success.

It is necessary to study and understand the mind's functions. Whosoever knows the mental mechanism is in a position to control it.

Much has been said about mental power and many are the schools that teach how to concentrate the mind. Nobody can intelligently deny the power of thought. This force is made up of radioactive forms and waves that move from one brain to the next. We need to develop this marvelous power but we must warn here that thought and action should wisely be combined if we want to succeed in life. Mental concentration is miraculous when intelligently combined with actions.

Mental power achieves prodigies and marvels when based on sincerity and the truth. Do not attempt to deceive your fellowmen. Do not use mental concentration to deceive your fellowmen, becatise failure for you will be inevitable. Mental power achieves prodigies when used to help others. By helping others we ourselves benefit. That is the Law.

Exercise

Do you need to succeed in something important? Sit in a comfortable chair, relax your muscles, concentrate on the business you are interested in. Imagine the business in full prosperity. Identify yourself with your fellowman; try to understand your fellowman's point of view; advise him mentally, making him see the advantages offered by that the business he is about to carry out with you. Thus, the mental waves will penetrate deeply in the other persons mind and will do marvels. One hour of perfect concentration is enough to determine success in a business.

Every merchant has the right to obtain money, but whatever you sell should be good, useful and necessary to others. Do not try to deceive others because you deceive yourself. Multitudes of peddlers travel the streets offering their merchandise uselessly. No one is interested in their merchandise. People become annoyed when they meet these peddlers. Their mistake is that they only think and talk about their wares. If they learned to see the point of view of others, they would inevitably succeed.

It is necessary to comprehend that all human beings have an "I" that wants to stand out, wants to make itself felt, to climb to the top of the ladder, etc.; this is precisely the human being's weakness. You also have that weak side. Do not fall into the same errors of others. Never say "I." Always say "we." Whoever masters himself can also master others.

Intelligently insinuate what you want, but do not say: "I want." Remember that others are not interested in what you want. Let others prepare your idea as if it was theirs. Provide the elements for that preparation, provide them very intelligently. Let others elaborate your ideas. People like to feel important; that is the weakness of the "I." Exploit that weakness. Never feel important and you will be important. Try to dissolve the "I" and you will be truly happy.

All success in life depends on the ability you have to deal with other persons. It is necessary to abandon egotism and to develop Christ-centrism. It is urgent to work for the common good. It is indispensable to dissolve the "I" and always think in terms of "we." The term "we" always has more power than the egotistical "I."

All the great failures of life are due to the "I." When the "I" wants to make itself felt, stand out, climb to the top of the ladder, then the reactions of others follow and the result of such mental reactions is failure. Remember that the "I" is energetic. The "I" is desire. The "I" is memory. The "I" is fear, violence, hatred, wants, fanaticisms, jealousies, distrust, etc. You need to explore profoundly all the depths of your mind because you have within you that which is called: "I, myself," the ego, etc.

If you want to succeed in life you should dissolve the "I." If you want to dissolve the "I," you should disintegrate all your defects. If you want to disintegrate your defects, do not condemn or justify them, comprehend them. When we condemn a defect, we hide it in the profound recesses of the mind. When we justify a defect, we strengthen it horribly. But when we comprehend a certain defect, we disintegrate it completely.

When the "I" is dissolved, we are filled with plenitude and happiness. When the "I" is dissolved, the Being, the Spirit, Love, expresses itself within and through us. Remember that God, the Spirit, the Inner Self of each man, woman and creature, is never the "I." The Being is divine, eternal and perfect. The "I" is Satan of Biblical legend. The "I" is not the body. The "I" is energetic and diabolic. In the "I" is the root of misery, poverty, failures, disillusionments, unsatisfied desires, violent desires, hatred, envy, jealousy, etc. CHANGE YOUR LIFE NOW! It is urgent that you understand the need to do away with all your defects, to dissolve the "I," Satan, the cause of all failures. When the "I" Is dissolved, only the Being, God, Happiness, remains in us. God Is Peace, Abundance, Happiness and Perfection.

Exercise

A man, after having studied himself, discovered that he had twelve defects that were bothering him. This man said, "Just as the hunter who tries to catch ten hares at once will not catch any, so is it also impossible to do away with my twelve defects at the same time."

This man arrived at the conclusion that it would be better to catch one hare and then another. First do away with one defect and then another. This man decided to dedicate two months to each defect. After twenty four months, this man no longer had the defects. He had done away with the twelve defects that hindered him from success. The result was marvelous. This man became the foremost citizen of the United States. His name: Benjamin Franklin.

Imitate this personage. Examine yourself and see how many defects you have. Count them, number them. Then dedicate two months to each defect, successively, until you eliminate all of them.

Sit in a comfortable chair. Pray to your Internal God like this:

> *You who are my true Being,*
>
> *You who are my Internal God,*
>
> *Enlighten me. Help me. Make me see my own defects.*
>
> *Amen.*

Concentrate until deep sleep arrives. Try to discover all your defects. We advise you to read the Bible. The word of the Divine Master is found in the four Gospels. There you will discover the virtues that you lack. Wherever a virtue is lacking, a defect exists.

May peace be with you!

Lesson Five

Money

Why has money assumed such an immense importance in our lives? Do we perhaps depend exclusively on it for our own psychological happiness? All of us human beings need food, clothing and shelter; this is understood. But why is it that this, which is so natural and simple for even the birds of the sky, has assumed such a tremendous and frightening importance and meaning?

Money has assumed such an exaggerated and disproportionate value because we psychologically depend on it for our well-being. Money nourishes our personal vanity, gives us social prestige, the means to achieve power. Money has been used by the mind for ends and purposes totally akin to those it has in itself, among which are to cover our immediate physical needs. Money is being used for psychological purposes; that is the reason why money has assumed an exaggerated and disproportionate importance.

We need money to have food, clothing and shelter; that is obvious. But when money becomes a psychological need, when we utilize it for different purposes than it has in itself, when we depend on it to obtain fame, prestige, social position, etc. then money assumes an exaggerated and disproportionate importance in the mind. This is where the struggle and the conflict to possess it originates.

It is logical that we have a need to obtain money to satisfy our physical needs (to have food, clothing and shelter). But if we depend on money for our own happiness and personal satisfaction, then we are the most wretched beings upon the earth. When we understand deeply that money only has as its purpose to provide us with food, clothing and shelter, we then spontaneously place an intelligent limitation on it. The result of this is that money no longer assumes the exaggerated importance that it has when it becomes a psychological need.

Money in itself is not good or bad. Everything depends on the use we give it. If we use it for good, it is good. If we use it for evil, it is evil.

We need to comprehend in depth the true nature of sensation and satisfaction. The mind that wants to comprehend the truth should be free of these obstacles.

If we truly want to free the mind of the obstacles of sensation and satisfaction, we must begin with those sensations which are more familiar to us, and there lay the adequate foundation for comprehension. Sensations have their suitable place, and when we comprehend them profoundly at all the levels of the mind they do not assume the stupid deformation they now have. Many people believe that if the order of things was according to the political party we belong to and for which we always struggle, that we would have a happy world, full of abundance, peace and perfection. That is a false concept, because none of that can exist if we have not previously individually comprehended the true significance of things. The human being is too poor internally and that is why he has a need for money and material things for his personal sensation and satisfaction. When one is poor internally, he externally seeks money and material things to complement himself and to find satisfaction. That is why money and things have assumed a disproportionate value and the human being is prepared to steal, exploit and lie at every instant. To this is due the struggle between capitalism and work, employers and employees, between exploiters and exploited, etc.

Useless are all the political changes if we have not first comprehended our own internal poverty. Economic systems can change again and again, the social system can be altered again and again, but if we have not profoundly comprehended the intimate nature of our inner poverty, the individual will always create new ways and means to obtain personal satisfaction at the expense of the peace of other people.

It is urgent to deeply comprehend the inner nature of this myself if we really want to be internally wealthy. Whoever is internally rich is incapable of exploiting his fellowman, he is incapable of stealing and lying. Whoever is internally wealthy is free of the obstacles of personal satisfaction and sensation. Whoever is internally wealthy has found happiness.

We need money, true. But it is necessary to profoundly comprehend our exact relationship with it. Neither the ascetic nor the covetous miser have ever comprehended our exact relationship with money. It is not through renouncing money nor coveting it that we can come to understand our exact relationship with it. We need comprehension to intelligently recognize our own material needs without disproportionately depending on money.

When we comprehend our exact relationship with money, the pain of detachment and the frightening suffering that is produced by competition ends.

We should learn to differentiate between our immediate physical needs and the psychological dependence on things.

The psychological dependence on material things creates exploitation and slavery.

We need money to cover our immediate physical needs. Unfortunately, needs are transformed into covetousness. The psychological "I," perceiving its own emptiness and misery, usually gives money and material things a different value, an exaggerated and absurd value, than what they truly have. That is how the "I" wants to become rich externally since he is internally poor and miserable. The "I" wants to make itself felt, to dazzle its fellowman with material things and money. Nowadays, our relationship with money is based on covetousness. We always allege necessity to justify covetousness. Covetousness is the secret cause of hatred and the brutalities of this world. Covetousness many times assumes a legal appearance. Covetousness is the cause of war and of all the miseries of this world. If we want to do away with the covetousness of the world, we should profoundly comprehend that this world is within our very selves. We are the world. The covetousness of the rest of the individuals lies within us. Actually, all individuals live within our own consciousness. The worlds covetousness is within the individual. Only by doing away with the covetousness that we carry within will covetousness in the world end. Only by comprehending the complex process of covetousness in all the levels of the mind can we experience the Great Reality.

Exercise

First: Lie down in the form of a star, opening your legs and arms to the left and the right.

Second: Concentrate now on your immediate physical needs.

Third: Meditate. Reflect on each of those needs.

Fourth: Lull yourself to sleep trying to discover on your own where necessity ends and where covetousness begins.

Fifth: If your exercise of concentration and inner meditation is done correctly, through internal vision you will discover which are your legitimate necessities and which are covetousness. Remember that only by profoundly comprehending necessity and covetousness will you be able to establish true foundations for the correct process of thinking.

Lesson Six

It is necessary that you have three things in life: food, clothing and shelter. We should not be hungry: we need to eat. We should not be poorly dressed: it is necessary to dress well. It is not fair to live our entire life paying apartment rent: we need to have our own good home. Reflect on all this. It is urgent for you to comprehend the need to live better without falling into the sin of covetousness.

In our previous lesson we said that it is necessary to distinguish between necessity and covetousness. It is necessary to know where necessity ends and where covetousness begins.

You need to learn how to make a good impression on other people. This is a very delicate art. Many ladies dress very well, sometimes with excessive luxury, and wear very valuable rings on their hands and yet, in spite of everything, they do not make a good impression on others. Many gentlemen wear very expensive suits and use the latest model cars and yet they fail many times because of not knowing how to make a good impression on people.

The President of Colombia, Dr. Olaya Herrera, controlled his people with his eternal smile; every smile of the president represented millions of dollars. We, the men, know that the smile of a woman is worth more to us than all the furs and diamonds that they use. A woman with a captivating smile causes a great impression among men.

The smile of sincerity and the perfume of courtesy achieve true miracles in the business world. It is urgent to distinguish between the smile of sincerity and the mechanical smile. The smile of sincerity comes from the very bottom of the soul. The mechanical smile is hypocritical and evil: it is the gesture of the devil.

In man there are two factors disagreeing: the soul and the devil. The soul is divine. The devil is malevolent. Every good action is of the soul. Every bad action is of the devil. When you knock on a door so that it will be opened, the head of the house can ask you many times: "Who is it?" Then you answer: "I." This "I," this myself, is precisely the devil in us. Clairvoyants see this "I" as a very horrible fluidic entity that lives within the human body. This entity also leaves the body during sleep and travels very far, wherever it is taken by its desires and passions.

The soul is not the "I." The soul is the Being. Distinguish between the Being and the "I." The Being is the soul. The "I" is Satan within us.

Your body does not think or desire. The body is only a suit, a robe. You think with the MIND. The mind is a vehicle of the soul. However, when we are evil, the mind becomes a vehicle of the devil. The diabolic mind wants wars, creates conflicts, problems, wants vices, alcoholic drinks, adulteries, fornication, covetousness, hypocrisy, etc.

The bee enjoys working. The ant is happy working. Learn to enjoy and derive pleasure from your job. When a store employee enjoys his work, he radiates mental waves of success and progress. Then the sales increase and the employer is happy with his employee and does not want him to leave. Be concerned about the success of the business where you work. It is necessary that you win over your employer's love. Learn to smile sincerely. Learn to enjoy work. If you want people to feel happy with you, it is necessary that you feel happy with others. If you do not feel happy with your job, if you do not want to smile, we advise you to listen to good music. Remember that music does miracles. Thus, you will also be able to change your character. When we listen to good music, when we spend long intervals listening to good music, we elevate our mind to higher levels of consciousness.

The mind radiates waves that travel through space. These waves pass from one brain to the next. A proof of the reality of these waves is found in telepathy. How many times do we walk on the street and all of a sudden the memory of someone strikes us and it so happens that we meet the very person we remembered? That is telepathy. That person's mental waves have reached us and we, at the same time, have received them.

We have an authentic wireless system in our organism. The pineal gland, situated in the posterior part of the brain, is the thought-transmitting center, and the solar plexus, situated in the umbilical region, is the receptive antenna. The pineal gland is the seat of the Soul, the window of Brahma. The soul enters and leaves the body through this window. The pineal gland is a small reddish-gray organ. This gland secretes a hormone which regulates the development of the sexual organs. After maturity, this gland degenerates into a non-secreting fibrous tissue. The pineal gland is the jigsaw puzzle of the wise, the thought-transmitting center. This pineal gland is developed in the great geniuses of science, art, philosophy, etc. It is totally atrophied in idiots. Great businessmen and individuals who usually have great success in their business commonly have this gland well developed.

The pineal gland is intimately related to the sexual organs. The strength of the pineal gland depends on sexual strength. The man or woman who foolishly wastes his or her sexual energy fails in business because their pineal gland becomes atrophied. A weakened pineal gland cannot forcefully radiate mental waves. The result is failure.

Be prudent. Do not waste your sexual energies foolishly. The Bible says: "Thou shalt not commit fornication." Fulfill this Sixth Commandment; save your sexual energies. By this means, you will fortify your pineal gland and inevitably succeed. In this manner, you will be able to radiate your mental waves with strength, power and glory. These mental waves, after having arrived at the receptive center (the solar plexus) of other people who come in contact with you, will give you the success that you seek. Be triumphant. Always smile full of sincerity. Live happily. Work with pleasure and happiness and the world will be yours; luck will smile on you from everywhere.

Exercise Before the Mirror

In front of a mirror, contemplate your face closely. Then pray:

My Soul, you should succeed;
My Soul, you should overcome Satan;
My Soul, take over my mind, my sentiments, my life.
You should keep the Guardian of the Threshold
    faraway from me;
You should overcome him;
You should take power over me totally.
Amen. Amen. Amen.

Say this prayer seven times and then observe in the mirror your eyes, your pupils, the center of your pupils, the retina of your eyes. Imagine them charged with light, strength and power. It is necessary that you try to mentally penetrate the interior of your eyes reflected in the mirror. It is necessary for you to try and see with your imagination, the center of those reflected eyes, the beauty of your soul. It is necessary for you to exclaim: "Oh my soul, I want to see you, I want to see you, I want to see you."

Intensely persevere, daily, with this exercise. Do your exercise every night before going to sleep. With this exercise you will develop clairvoyance. Practice for ten minutes daily. That is all.

Clairvoyance

It is necessary that you know that a sixth sense exists in us. That sixth sense is Clairvoyance. This faculty resides in the pineal gland. When you develop Clairvoyance, you will be able to read thoughts like reading from an open book. When you become clairvoyant you will be able to see the soul of people. When you become clairvoyant you will be able to see the "I" of people. Then you will comprehend that the soul is not the "I." The "I" is Satan in us. Clairvoyance allows us to see what lies beyond death. You will develop Clairvoyance totally with the exercises that we give you. You should practice these exercises. We want you to write us, communicating all your impressions to us.

May peace be with you!

Lesson Seven

Man faces innumerable problems in life. Each person needs to know how to solve each of these problems intelligently. We need to comprehend each problem. The solution of every problem is in the problem itself.

The time for us to learn how to solve our problems has arrived. Many problems exist: economic, social, moral, political, religious, family related, etc. and we should learn to solve them intelligently. The important thing to remember for the solution of every problem is to not become identified with the problem.

We have a certain tendency to become identified with the problem and the identification is so intense that we, in fact, become the very problem. The result of such identification is that we fail in the solution because a problem can never solve another problem.

One needs much peace and mental calm to solve a problem. An uneasy, battling, confused mind cannot solve any problem. If you have a very serious problem, do not become identified with the problem, do not become a problem yourself; retreat to any healthy recreational place: a forest, or a park, or the home of a very close friend, etc. Distract yourself with something different, listen to good music and then, with your mind tranquil and calm, in perfect peace, try to comprehend the problem profoundly, remembering that the solution to every problem is within the problem itself.

Remember that without peace you cannot do anything new. You need calm and peace to solve the problem which presents itself in your life. You need to think in a completely new way about the problem that you want to solve and this is only possible by having tranquility and peace. In modern life we have many problems, and unfortunately, we do not enjoy peace. This is a true jigsaw puzzle because we cannot solve problems without peace.

We need peace and we should study this in depth. We need to investigate the principal factor that puts an end to peace inside and outside ourselves. We need to discover what causes the conflict. The time has arrived to comprehend in depth at all levels of the mind the infinite contradictions which we have within, because that is the principal factor of discord and conflict. By comprehending in depth the cause of an illness, we cure the patient. Knowing in depth the cause of the conflict, we do away with the conflict: peace is the result.

Within and around us, thousands of conflict-forming contradictions exist. Truly, what exists within us also exists in society, because as we have said so many times, society is an extension of the individual. If there is contradiction and conflict within us, then these also exist in society. If the individual does not have peace, society will not have it either, and in these conditions all the pro-peace propaganda becomes, as a matter of fact, totally useless.

If we wisely analyze ourselves, we discover that a constant state of affirmation and negation exists within us. What we want to be and what we actually are: we are poor and we want to be millionaires, we are soldiers and we want to be generals; we are single and we want to be married; we are employees and we want to be managers, etc.

The state of contradiction engenders conflict, pain, moral misery, absurd actions, violence, murmuring, lies, gossip, etc. The state of contradiction can never bring us peace in life. A man without peace can never solve his problems. You need to intelligently solve your problems and therefore it is urgent that you have peace constantly. The state of contradiction impedes the solution of problems. Each problem implies thousands of contradictions. "Shall I do this? The other? How? When?" etc.

Mental contradiction creates conflicts and frustrates the solution of problems.

We first need to solve the causes of the contradiction in order to end the conflicts. Only in this manner will peace arrive, and with it the solutions of the problems. It is important to discover the cause of contradictions; it is important to analyze this cause in detail. Only in this manner is it possible to do away with the mental conflict. It is not correct to blame others for our internal contradictions. The causes of these contradictions are inside of us.

Mental conflict exists between what we are and what we want to be, between what a problem is and what we want it to be. When we have a problem of any type, either moral, economic, religious, family-related, marital, etc., our first reaction is to think about it, resist it, deny it, accept it, explain it, etc. It is necessary to comprehend that with mental anguish, contradiction, worry, conflict, it is not possible to solve any problem. The best way to react before a problem is silence. I am referring to the silence of the mind. This silence arrives by not thinking about the problem. The silence arrives when we comprehend that nothing is solved with conflict and contradictions. This silence is not a special gift of anyone, nor the capacity of a certain type. No one can cultivate this silence; it arrives by itself.

It arrives when we comprehend that no problem is solved by resisting it, accepting, denying, affirming or explaining it, etc.

From mental silence is born intelligent action, the intuitive and wise action which will solve the problem no matter how difficult it might be. This intelligent action is not the result of any reaction. When we perceive the event, the problem, when we notice the fact without affirming, denying or explaining it, when we do not accept the fact, nor reject it, then arrives the silence of the mind. Intuition flourishes in silence. From silence the intelligent action which totally solves the problem bursts forth.

Only in mental silence and calm is there freedom and wisdom.

Mental conflict is destructive and harmful. Mental conflict is a result of opposed desires: we want and we do not want, we desire this and the other. We are in constant contradiction and this, in fact, is conflict. The constant contradiction which exists within us is due to the struggle of opposite desires. There is a constant negation of one desire by another desire; one determination is replaced by another. A permanent desire does not exist in the human being; every longing is temporary. He wants a job and after he has it, he desires another job. The employee wants to be a manager; the priest wants to be a bishop. Nobody is satisfied with what he has. Everyone is full of unsatisfied desires and wants satisfaction.

Life is an absurd succession of fleeting and vain desires. When we profoundly comprehend that all the desires in life are fleeting and vain, when we understand that the physical body is engendered in sin and that its destiny is to rot in the grave, then true peace of the mind is born from that profound comprehension. Contradiction and conflict disappears. Only the mind that is in peace can solve problems. Peace rests in the silence of the mind.

Contradiction surges from obstinacy: when the mind clings to one single desire, when it wants its desire to be realized whatever it may cost, it is logical that there must be conflict. If we carefully observe two people who are discussing a problem, we will be able to confirm that each person clings to his desire, each person wants to see his desire satisfied, and this naturally creates mental conflict. When we resolutely see the vanity of desires, when we comprehend that desire is the cause of our conflicts and bitterness, true peace arrives.

Exercise

Seated in a comfortable chair, or lying down in your bed, close your eyes. Then concentrate on your interior, studying yourself, investigating your desires, your contradictions.

It is necessary for you to comprehend what your contradictory desires are, so that you may know in this manner the causes of your internal conflicts. Peace of mind comes from the knowledge of the causes of the mental conflict. Practise this simple exercise daily. It is necessary that you know yourself.

May peace be with you!

Lesson Eight

Alcoholism

This vice has three perfectly defined aspects:
1. Initiation
2. Intoxication
3. Death

Initiation

Some people begin this horrible vice during adolescence, others during their youth, others at maturity, and a few during old age. There are many causes that lead people to the vice of alcoholism. The adolescent that is initiated into this horrible path does it because he wants to feel like a complete man. He has a false concept of manhood. He believes that being a man means to be a drunkard, smoker, fornicator, adulterer, etc. The youngster reaches the crude vice of alcoholism, seduced by his friends or embittered by sufferings. Many times an amorous deception or a difficult economic situation tends to be the basic motive for initiating the fatal path of alcoholism. The mature man who joins this horrible path of alcohol does it, as usual, moved by the spring of his own bitterness; probably the death of a loved one, an amorous deception, a divorce, the loss of his job and his fortune, etc.

The human organism rebels against the first drinks. At the beginning the organism is not yet intoxicated and it is obvious that it strongly rejects the harmful ingredient of alcohol to which it is not accustomed.

Vomiting, an upset stomach after the huge drinking sprees, etc., are ways that the organism uses to eliminate the noxious ingredient. The fight of the organism is usually very violent but our malignant will proposes to violate it, and achieves it.

There is not a drunkard without his moral tragedy. The already intoxicated drunkard secretly guards his tragedy. The drunkard who is initiating himself in the vice always exteriorizes his tragedy, but when he comprehends that people do not understand him, he prefers to be silent.

Intoxication

Alcoholic intoxication comes once the defenses of the human organism have been overcome. On arriving at this second phase, the organism no longer feels well without alcohol. The intoxicated doctor can no longer carry out a surgical operation without his favorite drink; his pulse shakes, and if he carries out the operation, the results are very bad. The businessman can no longer do business without alcohol; he feels timid, nervous and fails. The worker is already incapable of working without his drink, he feels weak. Alcohol becomes a necessity for the intoxicated organism. The intoxicated one drinks and drinks, stimulated by the secret spring of his moral tragedy.

Some drunkards eat and drink; these last longer. Others do not eat so, as they say, "to not lose the intoxication"; these die very soon. Food favors the entire digestive system, but the lack of food definitely leaves the organism totally defenseless: the result is quick death.

Death

Every alcoholic intoxication concludes with death. Death can result from an ulcer or from cirrhosis of the liver or generally from any bad aspect of the liver, stomach, etc. It has been clinically proven that the drunkards that live longer are those who eat while drinking and that those who live short lives are those who do not eat while drinking.

The death of a drunkard is very horrible. They become very nervous in clinics and hospitals due to the lack of alcohol. They exclaim, shout, demand the bottle of alcohol; their desperation is frightening. Some die vomiting blood, others with terrible bloody diarrheas, etc.

Psychology of the Drunkard

The totally intoxicated drunkard spends everything on the vice. When the drunkard does not have anymore to spend, then he becomes a beggar, thief, swindler, or in the better of cases, nothing more than a simple slave of alcohol, a beggar of alcohol. The intoxicated one loses all concept of honor, dignity, responsibility, etc., and only one thing interests him in life: drinking. Alcohol becomes a vital fundamental necessity for the intoxicated person; that is all.

The serious things of life do not have any value for the drunkard; he is completely irresponsible. The intoxicated alcoholic is immoral in the most complete sense of the word. Dignity, word of honor, virtue, etc. have absolutely no importance for the intoxicated alcoholic. The hardhearted drunkard laughs at all those human qualities and even feels infinitely superior to his fellowmen.

Campaign Against Alcohol

The true effective campaign against alcohol is achieved by explaining with every detail the three defined aspects of this horrible vice, these three aspects of the path of alcohol: Initiation, Intoxication and Death. They should be pointed out at home, in school, at the university, in academies, temples, lodges, ashrams, sanctuaries, etc. This is the best way to effectively campaign against alcohol. Dry laws prohibiting the sale of alcohol are useless because drunkards then astutely invent their methods of making intoxicating drinks in a clandestine form. This does more harm than good to society. Only creative comprehension can save people from falling into this horrible and frightening vice. The audio-visual system of teaching is marvelous to combat the vice of alcohol.

The Home - True Education Begins at Home

Parents who drink set a bad example to their children, and lead their children down the fatal path of the Abyss. Children should be taught at home what this horrible vice is, the three aspects of this horrible path, etc. This type of teaching, accompanied by a good example, is radical in warning the new generation against the vice of alcohol.

Whatever is learned well at home is never forgotten.

Meditation and Intoxication

Meditation and intoxication are the opposite poles of the same force. Meditation is positive. Alcoholic intoxication is negative.

The Rosicrucian Gnostic should drink the wine of meditation in the sacred chalice of concentration. It is necessary to keep far away from the negative aspect. It is necessary to not fall into the negative aspect of the mind. The drunkard submerges himself into the atomic hells of nature and becomes lost in the Abyss. It is better to drink the wine of meditation in the sacred chalice of thought concentration. Let us concentrate our mind on our Inner God. Let us meditate on him for entire hours. In this manner we will reach Samadhi, the ineffable ecstasy. Then we will be able to converse with the Gods and penetrate the Great Mysteries of Nature. This is better than the "delirium tremens," which allows the drunkard to penetrate the atomic hells of Nature and be with the demons of the Abyss. The visions of the "delirium tremens" of drunkards are actually real; that which they see in their visions really exists. They see larvae, demons, and horrible monsters that really exist in the Atomic Infernos of Universal Nature. They penetrate the abyss and see the beings of the Abyss, perverse beings that live in the Atomic Infernos of Nature.

Alcoholic Larvae

Every human being carries around with him an atomic atmosphere perceptible to clairvoyants. These larvae live in the fourth dimension. By the way, we must say that modern physics already begins to admit the four coordinates, the fourth dimension, the fourth vertical. The drunkard carries in this ultra-sensitive atmosphere alcoholic larvae that stimulate him in the vice that gave them life, inciting him to drink. Said larvae only disintegrate with the fumes of sulphur.

Osmotherapy

Perfumes combined with mental power constitute a marvelous healing system. Drunkards can be healed by wisely combining these two elements.

Treatment

Do you have any loved one who is a victim of the vice of alcoholism? When he is asleep, hold his hand with your right hand. Make him smell a delicious perfume, a rose extract, and then talk to him with a soft voice as if he was awake. Advise him, explain to him in a detailed way what the horrible vice of alcoholism is. Remember that when the body sleeps, the ego leaves the body and travels in the fourth dimension.

The words you utter to the sleeping person reach the ear drum, go on to the brain's sensory center and are then transmitted to the ego even when the latter is far away from the physical body. On awakening, the ego returns to the physical body and if he does not remember what you told him, you can be certain that all you have said has remained in your loved one's subconsciousness. These words produce their effect little by little and the day finally arrives when the patient is cured of the horrible vice of alcoholism.

Exercise

Lie down and remain calmly in bed. Open your arms and legs to the right and left to form the Flaming Five-pointed Star. Relax your muscles properly. The process of relaxation is easy if combined with imagination. (Practice the exercise of relaxation in Lesson Two.)

Mental Relaxation

Once the relaxation of the physical body has been obtained, it is necessary to relax the mind. Mental relaxation is also obtained with the help of the imagination. Observe all the thoughts that come to mind, all the memories that assail you, all the worries, etc. Study them to find out their origin. The study of all this will reveal many things to you: it will make you get to know your defects, your errors, etc. In this manner, you will know how your "I," your ego, works.

Analyze each defect. Try to comprehend each defect in all the levels of the mind. Study each thought, memory or emotion which assails you. Comprehend each thought. Then imagine a profound abyss. Throw each studied thought, each memory, worry, etc. into that abyss.

In this manner, your mind will become silent and still. In the silence and calm of the mind you will be able to see and hear the Inner Self. He is the Internal Master. He is your Internal God.

Concentration

When the mind has achieved absolute calm and silence, it can concentrate on the Inner Self. This concentration is done with the help of prayer. Pray to your Inner Self. Try to converse with your Inner Self. Remember that praying is conversing with God. You can pray without formulae; in other words, talk to God: tell Him what your heart feels with infinite love.

Meditation

Whoever achieves perfect concentration can meditate on his Internal God. Reflect on your Internal God, identify yourself with him, and live in him.

Contemplation

Whoever learns to calm the mind, to concentrate the mind and pray, can practice perfect meditation and reach the heights of Internal Contemplation. On reaching these heights we are in ecstasy. We can talk face to face with the ineffable Gods, study the marvels of the infinite cosmos and travel through the infinite in Spirit and Soul. In that state of ecstasy the physical body remains asleep and abandoned. Now you will comprehend why it is convenient to practice these exercises during instances of drowsiness. Sleep is a faculty that should be taken advantage of to consciously achieve ecstasy.

May peace be with you!

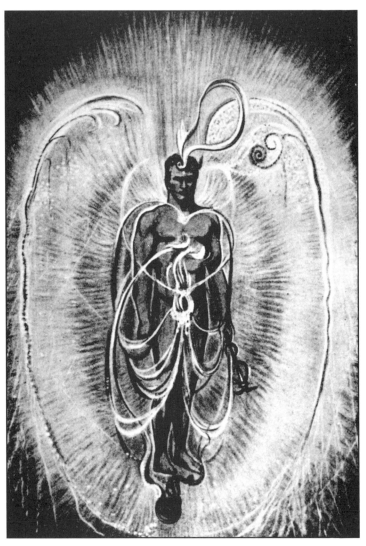

The economic and social problems of each person live in
the mind of everybody: no one is alien to another. We
are all in the mind of everybody else. The beggar lives
within the mind of the rich individual, and the rich one
lives in the mind of the beggar. We are all submerged in
the ocean of the Universal Mind.

Lesson Nine

The Universal Mind

Social living is based on the functions of the Mind. It is necessary to profoundly explore the diverse levels of the mind. The sphere of thought that man lives within is never locked up within the limited circumference of the cranium, as is generally supposed by the ignoramus and even the illustrious ignoramuses of the world. If such a man existed as those people believe, he would, of course, be the most unfortunate man in the world. A man with his mind imprisoned in his cranium could not see or perceive anything, he would be a complete idiot, living in the most profound darkness. That unfortunate creature would not see the Sun, the moon, stars, the earth we live in, people, things, nor light. Nothing that has existence would exist in the mind of such a man; this is explained by the fact that man can perceive nothing which does not exist beforehand in his own mind.

In his *Critique of Pure Reason* Immanuel Kant said, "The exterior is the interior." The entire Universe exists in the Cosmic Mind. The mental sphere of each person extends throughout the entire cosmos and reaches the most faraway stars. This is the cause of seeing, hearing and feeling all that is created. This is the reason for seeing the most remote stars. Our thoughts are not locked up in our cranium. Our mind extends throughout the entire cosmos. Our mind penetrates everywhere: worlds, suns, people and things; everything is within the mind of each man.

The Mind is Universal Energy. The Mind vibrates and sparkles in all creation. The cerebrum is not the mind. The cerebrum is only a receptive center, a radio-telegraphic office which receives the messages of the Mind. The cerebrum does not think. The one that thinks is the mind, and it is is not the cerebrum.

Religions say that the human Soul has a body of flesh and bones. The Theosophists maintain that besides the body of flesh and bones, the soul has a Mental Body. All the Oriental and Occidental schools dedicated to the study of Occultism teach their students how to use the Mental Body. The Soul dressed in the Mental Body can transport itself to other planets at will and see what happens there.

The entire Universe is within the human mind. All minds are within all other minds. We mutually live in the thought sphere of others. The economic and social problems of each person live in the mind of everybody: no one is alien to another. We are all in the mind of everybody else. The beggar lives within the mind of the rich individual, and the rich one lives in the mind of the beggar. We are all submerged in the ocean of the Universal Mind.

Imagination and Will

Imagination and Will are the two poles of the mind. The Imagination is feminine; the Will is masculine. The key to success is within the Imagination and Will united in vibrant harmony.

Mental Action

The inventor conceives with his Imagination the telephone, the radio, the automobile, etc., and then with the Will gives it shape, converts it into facts, into concrete reality. Parisian designers dictate fashions just as they conceive them in their Imagination.

Mental Epidemics

If a man thinks in both a good and a bad sense, the waves that emanate from his mind reach the Mental Body of each individual. Mental waves are propagated in all places. When the waves are those of wisdom and love, they benefit all those who receive them.

When the waves are permeated with devotion and veneration towards God, they carry peace and comfort to all those in suffering. Poisonous mental waves harm the mind of others. Mental waves of hatred, envy, covetousness, lust, pride, laziness, gluttony, etc. produce mental epidemics. Perverse mental waves poison many weak minds with their radioactivity.

The case of "rebels without a cause" is a good example of what mental epidemics are. The "rebels without a cause" have become an evil and harmful plague. The cause of this mental epidemic should be sought for in the ill-used imagination. Movie theatres show movies of bandits and gunmen which are then recorded in the minds of young people. Parents give their children guns, war trucks, tiny cannons, soldiers, toys, machine guns, etc. All of this is forcefully reflected in the imagination of children and adolescents. Then follow the magazines and comic books of police and robbers, pornographic magazines, etc.

The result of all this does not make itself wait; shortly afterwards, the child, the adolescent, actually becomes the "rebel without a cause," and later, the robber, the professional thief, the swindler, etc.

Mental Hygiene

It is necessary to practice mental hygiene. A preventive medicine is urgent. Develop wisdom and love. Pray a lot daily. Select works of art: we suggest good music, classical music, good paintings, the works of Michelangelo, the great operas.

Avoid spectacles harmful to the mind such as bloody spectacles like boxing, wrestling, bullfights, etc. These kinds of spectacles produce mental epidemics. Take care of your mind. Do not permit evil thoughts to penetrate the temple of your mind. Be pure in thought, word and deed. Teach your children all that is good, true and beautiful.

Origins of the Universal Mind

The great Divine Reality surged from its own bosom in the Aurora of this Solar Universe in which we live, move and have our own Being. The Great Reality does not know itself but, contemplating itself in the living mirror of the Great Imagination of Nature, it then comes to know itself. In this manner, a mental vibratory activity is created by which the Great Reality knows its infinite images that shine marvelously in the cosmic scenery.

This activity coming from the periphery going towards the center is called the Universal Mind.

All of us beings live submerged in the infinite ocean of the Universal Mind. Therefore, we all live in everyone else. No one can separate mentally. "The heresy of Separability is the worst of heresies."

The intelligent activity of the Universal Mind proceeds from a centripetal force and, since every action is followed by a reaction, the centripetal force, on finding a resistance in the center, reacts and creates a centrifugal activity called the Cosmic Soul. This vibratory Cosmic Soul turns out to be the Mediator between the center and the periphery, between the Universal Spirit of Life and Matter, between the Great Reality and its Living Images.

A Great Master said: "The Soul is the product of the centrifugal action of the Universal Activity impelled by the centripetal action of the Universal Imagination."

Terms

Centrifuge: is the force that tries to move away from the center. The force that goes from the center to the periphery.

Centripetal: the force which is attracted by the center. The force that flows from the periphery to the center.

Every individual can fabricate a Soul. When we know the technique of Internal Meditation, when we direct mental power to the interior of our own divine Center, the resistance that we will find internally will cause a reaction, and the more vigorous the centripetal force we apply, the more vigorous will be the centrifugal force which forms. Likewise do we fabricate a Soul. In this manner, the soul grows and expands. The strong and robust Soul incarnates and transforms the physical body: transforms it into more subtle and elevated manner until it also converts into Soul.

Exercise

Learn to use your Imagination and Will, united in vibrant harmony. Lying in your bed or seated in a comfortable chair, imagine a faraway place that you know well (a house, a park, an avenue, a city, etc.). Lull yourself to sleep with that image in your mind. When you find yourself falling asleep and with that image in your mind, fulfill that Imagination. Forget the place where your body is: put your Willpower into play and, full of self-confidence, walk in the imagined site. Walk in the imagined place as if you were there in flesh and blood. If the exercise is done correctly, you will leave your physical body and your soul will be transported to that place, where you will be able to see and hear everything that is happening there.

May peace be with you!

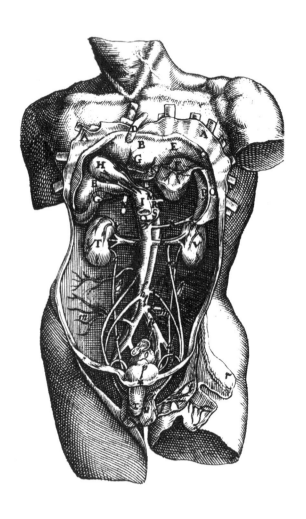

Appendix

The physical body is one of the marvelous instruments which man possesses to express himself. Considering this body from a strictly physical point of view, it is what we could call a machine, food being its combustible. The machine works and serves as an instrument according to the kind of combustible that is used.

Many times we meet people who radiate an attitude of bliss, happiness, health, optimism, sympathy, love, etc. These people win the friendship of everyone: they possess a force of attraction, a "magnet"; they are irresistible. Others are weak and lack that "magnet" which is so marvelous. They fail when they try to receive the help of other people, and when they are owners of a business their clients gradually leave them.

Psychology has discovered that a person's character depends on his internal state. Character does not develop in the physical body, but it expresses itself through it, and if the physical body is not in a good state, then our internal side cannot express itself efficiently.

It is indispensable that each person be nourished sufficiently. When nutrition is imperfect, the blood weakens and becomes poor, this being the reason why the cells also weaken. One of the best ways of obtaining complete nutrition with our customary food consists in perfectly masticating the delicacies. Food partially ingested loses a great part of its nutritional value.

Another point of great importance is the irrigation of the body: the proper use of water for the organism's benefit. The minimum amount of water required daily is two and a half liters. If water becomes scarce, then certain glands cannot function efficiently; the body does not eliminate all the wastes of the organism properly, the liver does not function well, etc.

Vegetarian Diet

The majority of people believe that food without meat is incomplete. Nothing is more erroneous because science has demonstrated that nutrition obtained from vegetables has a greater sustaining power.

All animals carry within the poisons of putrefaction. The venous blood is full of carbonic acid and other noxious substances. These harmful and repugnant substances are found everywhere in meat and when we eat these foods we fill our bodies with these toxins.

Abundant proofs exist which demonstrate that a carnivorous diet stimulates ferocity. Let us observe the ferocity of the beasts of prey and the cruelty of the cannibals, and compare them with the prodigious strength and docility of cattle, of the elephant, of the horse.

However, let us not jump to the conclusion that everyone should give up eating meat once and for all and dedicate themselves to vegetarian eating. It would be crazy for a person to change his ordinary diet which he has been using for years and which is nourishing him adequately. To eliminate meat from the ordinary diet of the people accustomed to it would completely undermine their health. The only sure way to proceed is by first experimenting and studying things.

You should be very careful with your nutrition. We do not ask you to give up meat once and for all but we do warn you that meat, when consumed in large quantities (for example, everyday), are like poison for the body. Dr. Arnold Krumm-Heller, Professor of Medicine of the University of Berlin and great Gnostic doctor, sustained that man should consume twenty percent of his food as meat.

We have verified that some foods such as wheat, eggs, avocados, etc. can substitute meat. Cereals, in general, are of great nutritive value. The protein of cow milk is marvelous. Milk from soybeans is very nutritious and its chemical composition is similar to that of cow milk.

Foods should be used in a balanced manner so as to obtain the best nutrition. Avoid eating white bread. White flour is harmful and does not contain any nourishment. Eat black bread, plantains, and corn flour instead of white bread and white flour. Eat many vegetables; remember that vegetables are fountains of great nourishment. Vitamins are found in vegetables.

May peace be with you!

Samael Aun Weor

How to Make the Light Within Ourselves

A Lecture by Samael Aun Weor

The Descent of the Ray of Creation

Note	Greek	Realm	Sephiroth	Laws
DO	Protocosmos	The Infinite	Ain Soph	1
SI	Ayocosmos	Spiritual Sun	Kether, Chochmah, Binah	3
LA	Macrocosmos	Galaxy	Chesed, Geburah, Tiphereth	6
SOL	Deuterocosmos	Solar System	Netzach	12
FA	Mesocosmos	Planet	Hod	24
MI	Microcosmos	Physical Body	Malkuth	48
RE	Tritocosmos	Inferior Worlds	Klipoth	96 +

All creation unfolds according to the Law of Seven, the Law of the Octave: Do-Re-Mi-Fa-Sol-La-Si. Thus when the Light of the Christ descends and creates, everything is organized in seven stages. These notes descend from perfection, thus the author follows the notes downward from DO. The process of the unfoldment of this light is known as the Ray of Creation or the Ray of Okidanokh. It is the Cosmic Christ.

How to Make the Light Within Ourselves

Moses writes in *Genesis*:

"Let there be light:" and there was light. - Genesis 1:3

This is not something related with a remote past, no. This tremendous principle does not change through time; it is as eternal as eternity; it is a tremendous reality that exists from instant to instant, from moment to moment.

Let us remember Goethe, the great German initiate; his last words moments before his death were "Light, more light."

Goethe is reincarnated in Holland. He has a physical body; now he does not have a masculine body, he has a feminine one and is married with a Dutch prince, and is now a Dutch lady of the high society. This is very interesting, is it not?

Well, as I was saying, the light is very important. Meanwhile one lives in the darkness; one will have to yearn the light because one is blind. The light is the maximum desire for a person that is living in a cave, for one that lives underground amidst the darkness.

Indeed, the Essence is the most honourable and the most decent thing that we have inside. Originally it comes from the Milky Way where it vibrates with the musical note La, when descending it has to pass through the Sun with the musical note Sol. It enters this physical world (the physical body) with the note Mi.

The Essence is beautiful. It is, we would say, a fraction of the human-Christic principle that everyone has inside. It is the Human Soul that normally lives in the Causal World. For this reason it is correct to say that the Essence is Christic, and that our Consciousness in Christ will save us, etc., etc., etc.

All of that is true, but the problem with our Consciousness is that it, being so precious, having so many marvellous virtues, precious natural powers, is trapped among all those undesirable subjective elements that unfortunately we carry within ourselves; that is to say, is imprisoned in a dungeon. The Essence wants the light. How? Yearning it! There is not one person that would not want the light, unless that person is already lost, but when one has some aspiration, one yearns for the light.

Therefore, one has to make the light. To create the light is something very serious because it means the destruction of the receptacle or dungeon. This means to rescue, to liberate, to take the Essence out from the black den where is imprisoned. Only then one will be as one should be: as an illuminated person, an authentic clairvoyant, a real luminous being that enjoys the plenitude which by nature belongs to us, and that we have the total right to possess.

However, it happens that one needs heroism or a number of tremendous heroic acts in order to liberate the Soul, to take it out from the dungeon, from the darkness where it is imprisoned.

It would be good if you could really comprehend in a conscious way what I am saying here, because it can happen that even while listening, you do not really listen, or that you will not feel the sense of the words that I am saying.

The light that shines in the darkness like a star of six rays in a nocturnal sky comes from our spermatic Chaos.

It is beautiful to rescue the Soul from the darkness but it is not easy. The normal situation for the Essence is to stay imprisoned. One will be unable to enjoy authentic illumination meanwhile the Essence, the Consciousness, the Soul, is trapped, imprisoned, and that is serious. Therefore, it is necessary, mandatory, to destroy the **Ego** with an heroism superior to Napoleon and his great battles, superior to the fights of Morelos in his struggle for freedom, etc., in order to liberate the poor Soul, to take it away from the darkness.

First of all, it is necessary to know the techniques, the procedures that lead to the destruction of those elements in which the Soul is trapped, imprisoned, so illumination can be attained.

Self-observation

The very beginning of this is to understand the necessity to know how to **observe**. We, for example, are all sitting down in these chairs, we know that we are sitting, but we have not **observed** these chairs. In the first case, we have the **knowledge** that we are sitting in the chair, but to observe it, this is already something different.

In this case there is, I would say, knowledge but no observation; true observation requires a special observation: to observe what things are made of, and then to submerge oneself in meditation in order to discover thier atoms, molecules; this requires **Directed Attention**. To know that one is sitting in a chair is a Non-Directed Attention, passive attention, but to observe the chair is Directed Attention.

In the same way, we can think a lot about ourselves, but this does not mean that we are observing our own thoughts; to observe them is different.

We live in a world of inferior emotions; anything can generate an inferior emotion in us. We can know that we have them, but it one thing is to know and another to observe the negative state in which one is; that is something completely different.

Let us see an example. On a certain occasion, a gentleman said to a psychologist, "Well, I feel antipathy for a certain person" (he said the name).

The psychologist answered, "You have to observe. Observe that person."

The gentleman asked, "But what do I have to observe him for, if I already know him?"

The psychologist arrived at the conclusion that this person did not want to observe; he "knew," but was not *observing*.

To know is one thing, and to observe is something absolutely different. One can know that one has a negative thought, but it does not mean that one is observing it. One knows that one is in a negative state, but one has not observed the negative state.

In practical life, we see that within ourselves there are many things that give us reason to feel ashamed: ridiculous comedies, grotesque inner things, morbid thoughts, etc. To know that one has these things is not same as to have observed them.

Somebody could say, "Yes, in this moment I have a morbid thought." It is one thing to know that one has a morbid thought, and another to observe the thought.

If one wants to eliminate a particular undesirable psychological element, first of all one has to learn to observe with the intention of attaining a transformation, because certainly, if one does not learn to Self-observe, any possibility of transformation is rendered impossible.

When one learns to Self-observe, one develops the sense of Self-observation. Commonly, this sense is atrophied in the human race, it is degenerated; but according with its use, it develops and unfolds.

Firstly, through Self-observation we can verify that the most ridicules comedies and even the most insignificant thoughts that appear internally and that are never externalized are created by others, by the "I's." It is a serious thing for one to become identified with those comedies, with that ridiculousness, with those protests, with that anger, etc. If one is identified with any of those inner extremes, the "I" that produced them becomes stronger and in this way any possibility of elimination becomes more and more difficult. So, observation is vital when we want to produce a radical transformation within ourselves.

Through the Hermetic Work, we crystallize what before was diffused in the sinister and vulgar mass of the "I's."

The different "I's" that live within our psyche are very astute, very smart. Many times they use the memories that we carry in the intellectual center. Let us suppose that in the past, we fornicated with a person of the opposite sex and that now, we are trying (or not trying) to eliminate the lust. The "I" of lust will use the center of the memories, the intellectual center, and will take the memories that it needs and will make them into a fantasy of the person, so the "I" will become stronger. Each time it will become stronger.

For all of this, you have to see the necessity of Self-observing. Radical and definitive change is not possible if we do not learn to observe ourselves.

To know does not mean to observe. To think does not mean to observe, either. Many people believe that to "think" in oneself is to observe, but it is not. One can be thinking in oneself, however this is not observing. To think in oneself and Self-observation are as different as the net and water or water and thirst.

Obviously, one must not be identified with any of the "I's." In order to perform Self-observation, one has to divide oneself in two, in two halves; one part that observes and the other that is observed. When the part that observes sees the ridiculousness and stupidities of the observed part, there are great possibilities to discover (suppose the "I" of anger) that this "I," is not us, that he is he. We could exclaim then, "The 'I' of anger is an 'I,' it has to die; I will work on it in order to disintegrate it!"

But if one is identified with the defect and says, "I have anger, I am furious!" then the defect becomes stronger, and in this condition, how could we eliminate it? Well, it would not be possible. Therefore, one must not be identified with that "I," with its rage or with its tragedy, because if one is identified with one's own creation (the "I"), one ends up living his own creation, and that is something absurd.

According to one's work on oneself, as one advances deeper in the field of Self-observation, one's observation becomes more and more profound. In this work, one should not overlook even the most insignificant thought; any desire, even if it is transitory, any reaction, has to a motive of observation, because any desire, any reaction, any negative thought, comes from a particular "I." If we want to make light, to liberate the Soul, will we allow the existence of those "I's"? That would be absurd! If light is what we want, if we are really in love with the light, then we have to disintegrate the "I's." There is no other solution but to reduce to dust what we have observed in ourselves; therefore, we need to know how to observe ourselves.

Chatter

In this field, we have to be careful with **Inner Chatter**, because there are many negative and absurd inner dialogues; there are many inner talks that never end. Naturally, we need to correct that situation. To learn to be silent, to know to speak when it is necessary to speak, to know to keep silent when it is necessary to be quiet (this is law not only for the physical world, the external world, but also for the inner worlds).

The negative Inner Chatter, when exteriorized physically, is harmful. This is the reason why it is so important to eliminate that negative aspect; it is necessary to learn to keep internal silence.

Normally, Mental Silence is defined as emptying the mind of any class of thoughts, as when one achieves the quietude and silence of the mind through meditation, etc. However, there is another type of Silence. Let us suppose that there is presented to us a case of critical judgement, a case that is related to someone else, and we keep a mental silence; we do not judge, we do not condemn, we remain silent externally and internally; in this case, there exists Inner Silence.

The facts of practical (external) life are in intimate relation with perfect inner behavior. When the facts of practical life are in harmony with perfect inner behaviour, it is a clear signal that we are creating within ourselves the famous Mental body.

Inside of each one of those different quarrelsome and bawling "I's" that personify our psychological errors exist a substance: the psychic Essence. As the splitting of an atom liberates energy, so in the same way the total disintegration of the different infernal "I's" liberates Essence, Light. So, we have to make light.

If we put different parts of a radio or of a tape recorder on a table but do not know anything about electronics, we would not be able to receive the different soundless vibrations that fill the cosmos. But if through comprehension we connect the different parts, we will have a radio, we will have the instrument that can perceive sounds that we could not otherwise perceive. In the same manner, the different parts of these studies, of this work, complement each other in order to form a marvellous body: the famous Body of the Mind. This body will let us perceive in a better form all that exists within us and will develop even more the sense of inner Self-observation. That is very important!

So, the object of observation is to produce a change within us, to promote an authentic and effective change.

Once we have become skilfull in the observation of ourselves, then comes the process of elimination.

There are three steps or stages in this matter: first, the observation; second, the critical judgement, and the third is the elimination of a particular psychic "I."

"I's" in the Five Centers

Once we are observing an "I," first we have to see its behavior in the intellectual center to know all its games in the mind; second, how it expresses itself through the feelings in the heart; and third, to discover its way of action in the inferior centers: motor, instinctive and sexual.

Obviously, an "I" expresses in one way through the sexual center, in another way through the heart, and in yet another way through the brain.

In the brain, an "I" expresses itself through the intellect: reasons, justifications, subterfuges, evasions, etc.

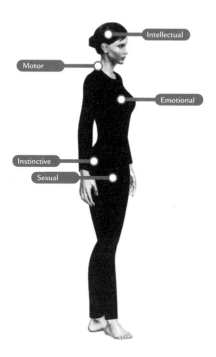

In the heart, it may express as a suffering, as an affection, and many times as an apparent love, even when it is just lust, etc.

In the motor-instinctive-sexual centers, it will have another form of expression: as action, as an instinct, as a lascivious impulse, etc.

For example, let us take a concrete case: lewdness or lasciviousness. A lustful "I," in front of a person of the opposite sex, can express itself in the mind as constant thoughts. It could appear in the heart as an apparently pure love, without any stain, such that one could justify oneself and say, "Well, I do not feel lewdness for this person, what I am feeling is love." But if one is sensitive, if one pays attention to the human machine and observes the sexual center, one discovers that in the sexual center there is some activity in relation to that person. Then we verify that it is not affection, that there is no real love, but only lust.

But let us observe how slender is the crime: the lust can be perfectly concealed in the heart as love, to write poems, etc., but it is concealed lust. If one is careful and observes the five centers of the machine, then one can verify that is an "I."

When we have already discovered that it is an "I," when we have known its behavior in the five centers, in the intellectual, in the heart and in the motor-instinct-sex, then one can pass to the third stage. What is the third stage? The elimination; that is the final stage of the work. Then one has to use Prayer in the Work. What do we understand about Prayer in the Work? Prayer in the Work has to be practised having as foundation Inner **Self-remembering**.

In certain occasions we said that there are four levels of men, or Four States of Consciousness.

The First State of Consciousness is the profound and unconscious dream of a person, of an ego that left the body sleeping on the bed, but that walks in the Molecular World in a comatose state; that is his inner state.

The Second State of Consciousness is the one of the dreamer who has returned to the physical body and believes that he or she is in a "waking state." In this case the dreams remain, for sure, but the person is with the physical body in a waking state, this second type of dreamer is more dangerous because he can kill, he can steal, he can commit crimes of any kind.

The Four States of Consciousness

	Gnostic	Greek	Description
The Consciousness is completely awake.	Fourth State	Nous	Objective, awakened consciousness; Objective Clairvoyance. Intuition. Samadhi. There is no dreaming in this state.
The Consciousness is awake in some percentage.	Third State	Dianoia	Self-remembering; continual directed attention, constant penetrating Self-observation; inner seperation from thoughts, feelings and sensations. Accompanied by conceptual analysis, revision of beliefs, etc.
Consciousness is asleep.	Second State	Pistis	The so-called "Vigil State." Marked by beliefs, concepts, ideologies, opinions, prejudices, theories, fanaticism, etc. Common humanity never rises above this state.
	First State	Eikasia	Physical sleep; Marked by brutality, animal passion, cruelty, instinctive desire.

In the first case, the dreamer is more infra-human, but cannot do any of those things. How could he? How could he damage somebody? When the body is passive to the dreams, the person cannot damage anybody in the physical world, but when the body is acting out the dreams, the person can create a lot of damage in the physical world. So that is why the sacred Bible emphasises the necessity of **awakening**.

These two types of persons are in state of profound unconsciousness. If they pray while within those two types of infra-human states, nothing good can be expected. However, nature will answer. For example, an unconscious person, a dreamer, goes to pray in order to get a deal, but it can happen that among those many "I's," some do not agree with what the dreamer is asking for, because the prayer is for just one of those "I's"; the other "I's" were not taken into consideration. Therefore, it could happen that the other "I's" do not feel any interest in that deal and do not agree with that prayer, and pray exactly the opposite in order to make that deal fail. Because they disagree, because the other "I's" are the majority, nature answers with its forces, with a flow of forces, and the deal fails; that is clear!

Then, in order to get an effective result with Prayer in the Work on ourselves, one has to use the Third State of Consciousness, the Inner Self-remembering of our own Being.

Submerged in a profound meditation, concentrated in the Inner Divine Mother, one will supplicate her to eliminate from the psyche the "I" that one wants to disintegrate. It could happen that the Divine Mother in that moment might act beheading that "I," but this does not mean that the totality of the work has been done. The Divine Mother will not disintegrate everything instantaneously. It will be necessary to be patient. In successive works, through time, we will get the slow disintegration of that "I"; it will lose size and volume.

An "I" can be frightfully horrible, but in accordance to its lost volume it becomes more beautiful; then it takes the aspect of a child and finally becomes dust. When it is reduced to dust, the Consciousness that was trapped, imprisoned, inside of that "I," is liberated, and the percentage of light within ourselves is increased. It will be a percentage of light that is free. In this manner we will proceed with each one of those "I's."

The Work is long and very hard; many times a negative thought, even being an insignificant one, is originated by an ancient "I." The negative thought that comes to the mind indicates that there is an "I" inside of the thought, and that "I" has to be extirpated, eradicated from our psyche.

It is necessary to study and to know its conduct, to see how it behaves in the five centers: in the intellectual, in the emotional, and speaking in synthesis, in the motor-instinctive-sexual; to see how it works in each one of these Three Brains. According to how the "I" behaves, one gets to know the defect.

When one has developed the sense of Self-observation, one can verify that some of those "I's" are frightfully horrible, real monsters of horrifying and macabre forms that live within our psyche.

Matrimony, Divorce and Tantrism

If I speak with the tongues of men and of angels, but have not love, I am become sounding brass or a clanging cymbal.

And if I have prophecy, and know all mysteries and all knowledge, and if I have all faith, so as to remove mountains, but have not love, I am nothing.

And if I shall dole out all my goods in food, and if I deliver up my body that I may be burned, but have not love, I profit nothing.

Love has long patience, is kind; love is not emulous [of others]; love is not insolent and rash, is not puffed up, does not behave in an unseemly manner, does not seek what is its own, is not quickly provoked, does not impute evil, does not rejoice at iniquity but rejoices with the truth, bears all things, believes all things, hopes all things, endures all things.

Love never fails...

- 1 Corinthians 13

Matrimony, Divorce, and Tantrism

The decadence of good customs in countries that boast of being civilized is lamentable. The civil or religious formula of matrimony has been converted into a legal permit in order to fornicate for a few days, after which the couple gets a divorce. So, they marry today and divorce tomorrow. That is all.

In this day and age, instead of saying, "Let's go and sleep together," the perverse say, "Let us get married." Thus, this is how, by legalizing lewdness, perverts dissimulate or hide their shame a little.

Practically speaking, modern laws have converted matrimony into a new type of prostitution. We know the case of women who have been married ten or fifteen times; many of these ladies are great movie celebrities, or ladies of high society, yet nobody says anything against their ten or fifteen husbands, because when this type of prostitution has been legalized, everyone in the whole world keeps their mouth shut.

Indeed, people mistake passion for love. Passion is a poison that cheats the mind and the heart. The impassioned man firmly believes that he is in love. The impassioned woman could even swear that she is in love.

The impassioned ones dream of love, they sing to love, however they have never awakened to the world of love. They do not know what love is; they only dream of it and believe they are in love; that is their mistake. Thus, when their passion has been completely satisfied, only the cruel reality remains; then they end in divorce.

It may seem to be an exaggeration, but the fact is that out of a million couples who believe that they are in love, only one couple is really in love. Millions of impassioned couples exist, yet couples in love are very difficult to find.

It is urgent to dissolve the "I" in order to build the Soul. Only the Soul knows how to truly love. The Soul is strengthened and fortified with the fire of the Holy Spirit. It is good to know that the fire of the Holy Spirit is love. It is also good to know that the fire of the Holy Spirit is the Kundalini of which the Hindustanis speak. Only this flaming sexual fire can open the Seven Churches of the Soul. Only this electronic fire can fill the Soul with igneous powers. Whosoever does not understand this can lose the Soul; the Soul who renounces sex and love inevitably dies.

A man shows his virility by performing deeds of love, not by talking about a love that he is incapable of accomplishing.

The kiss of the Mother Kundalini is for the virile man and for the woman who is truly in love with her husband. The kiss of the Mother Kundalini is death. The kiss of the Mother Kundalini is life. Those who are impassioned know nothing about these things. They only think of how to satisfy their desires and then they get divorce, without another thought, this is the only thing they know to do; wretched people... they are worthy of pity!

Bake and re-bake and re-bake your clay and your water again, so that when your clay returns to the clay and your water evaporates, only your Amphora of Salvation remains, in other words, only your resplendent and sparkling Soul remains in the hands of your Inner God.

The one who sees a sin within love, the one who hates sex, is a degenerated infrasexual who wants to castrate the Sun, yet, for his disgrace, he will be castrated. Whoever hates love and sex will not consume the food of the Sun and his testicles will dry up and die before his death. (Editor: The Sun is the cosmic Christ, the source of Life).

Those who believe they are in love must make a dissection of their "I," they must self-explore themselves with the goal of discovering if what they have within their heart is passion or love. Thus, lovers need to know themselves in order to not become emasculated, and to make their creation with virility. If your love is one, and if all loves are included within your love, then your testicles will consume the food of the Sun. Whosoever wants to enter into the Kingdom of Esotericism must garb themselves with the Garment of Regeneration; this is the Wedding Garment.

At the table of the guests, where the Angels sit, one cannot enter without a Wedding Garment. This Garment cannot be attained by those who spill the sacred wine. The few who are really in love know that the wine must not be spilled. Unfortunately, true lovers are very rare... they hardly exist.

Judas is never missing within matrimonies. The fatal triangle, adultery, is the cause of thousand of divorces. It seems incredible, but in fact, even the Great Arcanum is now utilized by the tenebrous ones in order to commit adultery and to satisfy their passions. Even that which is most sacred is profaned by the adulterers and fornicators. Perverts do not respect anything.

Happiness in matrimony is only possible with the death of Judas. This Judas is the "I," the "myself," the reincarnating ego.

We have to unite Peter and John. First, we have to tread the path of Peter and to work with the Philosophical Stone (sex). Thereafter, we have to arrive at the path of John (the Word). These two paths are separated by a frightful abyss where only weeping and gnashing of teeth are heard. We need to extend a bridge in order to unite the two paths, if indeed we want to go from Peter to John. The name of that bridge is death. Here is where Judas, the "I," the "myself," the ego, must die.

Remember that the kiss of the Mother Kundalini is death and resurrection. One day you will awaken, and then you will have the joy of dying within yourself. Judas must die on the bridge, if you want to arrive at the path of John (the Word). It is necessary for you to be dead so that you can become free. Thus, convert your clay into an Amphora of Salvation (Soul) within which the great, hidden Lord can pour that food, that drink, which is the unique solar food and the unique solar drink. This is how anyone who victoriously achieves the escape from the horrendous valley of death can satiate his hunger and thirst for justice.

Peter, who is by interpretation Cephas, a stone, represents the entire work with sex. John signifies the Word, the incarnation of the Word through successive degrees and successive cosmic initiations.

As Christ, Peter is also crucified, yet with his head aiming downwards, towards the stone; this indicates to us the work with the Philosophical Stone (sex). John (the Word) rests his head on the heart of the Christ Jesus as if saying, "Provide me a refuge of love within thine home, and I shall return to you this love made eternal within my Sacred Heart."

However, everyone must build the bridge by themselves. Then, by means of the death of Judas, the path of Peter is united to the path of John. Only by arriving to John can the Word become flesh, become Self-realized within us, and we Christify ourselves. Yet not all comprehend the path of Peter, thus they do not walk on it, because they still do not know that stones have heart. Thus, they do not comprehend the path of John either. No one can arrive at the path of John without having walked the path of Peter (Sex). John (the Word) is waiting for us.

Let us remember the scene on the sea of Tiberias after they had dined on fish; Peter, seeing John, said to Master Jesus, "Lord, and what shall this man do?" and Jesus answer him, *"If I will that he tarry till I come, what is that to thee? Follow thou me."* - John 21:21-22

Indeed, the Word is waiting in the bottom of our Ark for the moment of its realization. The Perfect Matrimony is the path of Peter, yet we need to extend the bridge of death in order to arrive at the path of John. Judas, the "I," is the one who damages the happiness of matrimonies. Judas fornicates and gets married because of animal passion, yet he believes he is in love. So, we need to hang Judas on the bridge of death. Only thus can we arrive to John. Regeneration is impossible without the death of Judas (the "I").

Sex is not only mind; even the stones have a heart, and if we want to make sex only mental, we violate the Law and commit adultery; the outcome will be a total failure, the abyss, and the Second Death.

Judas betrays us from moment to moment; we will never arrive at the path of John. When people resolve to die from moment to moment, then happiness will reign in all homes and fornication and adultery will end.

Divorced people are the outcome of passion. Thus, when passion is dead, mistaken matrimonies and divorce cannot exist.

There also exist those who get married purely because of economical interests or common conveniences; this is how Judas sells the Christ for thirty silver coins. The outcome is divorce.

In this day and age, money marries money, and imbecilic people state, "The more you have, the more you are worth; money talks."

This is how the insulters, the blasphemers against the Holy Spirit, talk; they believe they are practical people, thus they constantly get married and divorced (if they are lucky enough not to be killed by the resentful ex-spouse). Indeed, these people totally ignore that which is called love. Nonetheless, they talk of love and even swear eternal love.

Magazines and other modern love advertisements, etc., are now in fashion. Absurd advertisements of this kind are abundant. i. e., "White woman, such height, such capital, eyes of this or that color, with this weight and this religion, etc., wishes to marry a gentleman with this or that age, with this quantity of money, this race, this height, etc."

"A gentleman, of such height, such capital, eyes of this or that color, with this weight and this religion, etc., wishes to marry a woman with this or that age, with this quantity of money, this race, this height, etc." all of this is indeed very absurd and horrible. All of this is nothing but prostitution authorized by the authorities and society. The outcome of this is suffering, absurd matrimonies, prostitution and divorce.

Good customs are lost, and unity within homes has hit rock bottom. In this day and age, married people go around alone within night clubs, taverns, cinemas, etc. Saturdays are very special days for these married people; on weekends, married people bountifully squander their money within taverns and miserably adulterate, without caring at all for the fate of their children.

Men and women have delivered themselves to the debauchery of good customs, thus the outcome cannot be anything but the failure of their matrimonies. What is built upon a false basis becomes false. To be married based upon passion, to be married based upon economical interests, based upon social conveniences, etc., leads to an inevitable failure.

In order for love to exist, the complete, mystical communion of man and woman is necessary in all the levels of their minds. If in the seven levels of the Being there is not a complete communion, then the outcome is divorce.

Love is like a solitary tree that is illuminated by the Sun. Love is like a newborn child. Love is like an ineffable rose bathed by the light of a full moon. Love and passion are incompatible. Love and passion are two substances that cannot be combined. Love is absolutely innocent. Where there is love, jealousy, anger, and resentment cannot exist, because love is incompatible with all of those lower passions.

Love begins with a flash of delectable sympathy. It is substantiated with the force of tenderness, and it is synthesized in adoration. A Perfect Matrimony is the union of two beings: one who loves more, and the other who loves better.

Before getting married, it is necessary to self-explore our "I" very sincerely and profoundly, in order to totally self-discover our selves. We must use the scalpel of self-criticism to extract the passion we have within, and place it on the carpet of crude reality.

At times it is better to know how to renounce, instead of failing lamentably. It is urgent to discover if indeed the plentitude of love exists within us.

Only on the basis of love can we have a good matrimony. In order for love to exist, there must be affinity in thought, affinity in sentiments, affinity in emotions, affinity in action, affinity in religion, and affinity in ideas, etc. Where this mystical communion is missing, love is impossible.

Regarding this subject-matter of matrimony, legislators can establish all the laws they wish, nevertheless, indeed, they will achieve nothing, because happiness within matrimony is only possible when we hang Judas (the "I"). Thus, whosoever wants to be happy in their marriage must be sincere with themselves and not marry because of passion, because of money or because of social status.

Modern matrimonies corrupt the sexual act. Modern matrimonies have failed because of sexual abuse. Modern matrimonies do not want to comprehend the divine majesty of sex. It is necessary to know that sex is very sacred. In the sacred India of the *Vedas*, sex is utilized in order to achieve more elevated states of Samadhi (ecstasy).

Amongst the Hindustani Yogas, sex is utilized in order to attain the union (Yug) with the Spirit-essence and thus the entrance into Nirvana. Not a single sage of the East would ever conceive of the idea of utilizing sex purely for carnal passion. The White Tantric Yogis perform sex with their spouse in order to attain Inner Self-realization.

The best of Hinduism and Buddhism is White Tantra. The best of Yoga is Sex Yoga.

Tantrism

We can assert that Tantrism is the essence of Yoga. There exist three types of Tantrism: white, black and grey. Indeed, White Tantrism is unique and worthwhile, because neither the orgasm nor the ejaculation of semen exist in it.

White Tantrism awakens the Kundalini, in other words, the fire of the Holy Spirit. That fire fortifies the soul; it strengthens it and fills it with terribly divine igneous powers.

Sex Yoga states, "Poison must be transformed into medicine." They understand by poison the lure of women and of spirituous beverages. In alchemical terms, we would say that it is necessary to transform lead into gold.

Indeed, Yoga is worthless without Tantrism. Yoga is worthless without its sexual essence.

Brahmins consider the sexual union as equivalent to a divine sacrifice, and the feminine organs as the fire where the sacrifice is offered. The Brahmin woman says the following in one of sacred texts: "If your objective is to utilize me for sacrifice, let it be granted unto thee any blessing that through my mediation thou summon."

Buddhist Tantrikas attain Nirvana by means of the woman and sex. Yogis and Yoginis reach Samadhi (ecstasy) through the sexual act without spilling the semen. This is the *coitus reservatus*, in other words, the sexual act without reaching the orgasm, without ejaculating the semen.

The Tantric Yogis and Yoginis pass through a long and difficult preparation before entering in to the field of Sex Yoga. This entire preparation requires concentration, meditation, bandhas, mudras, pratyahara, pranayamas, etc. One text indicates that the Yogi has

When you make male and female into one...
then you will enter into the Kingdom.

- Jesus, from *The Gospel of Thomas*

to sleep for three months with the Yogini to his right and another three months to his left, without having sexual intercourse with her. The sexual intercourse without ejaculation is performed only after the two periods of three months. This act is named or called Maithuna. Nirvana is achieved with Maithuna. Samadhi (ecstasy) is attained with Maithuna. The Kundalini awakens and develops totally with Maithuna. Yogi and Yogini begin the dance of Shiva and Shakti (the eternal feminine and her spouse), thus they happily dance before the Tantric sexual act.

Thus, after the sacred dance the Yogi and Yogini couple sit to meditate as the Mayan Initiates do, back against back, the two dorsal spines making contact in order to achieve perfect mental and emotional breathing dominion.

They sit in the oriental style on the ground, with their legs crossed, as the Buddha is represented. The practice of Maithuna is performed only after this. Amongst the Yogis, all of this is performed under the guidance of a Guru. The Guru performs great, powerful magnetic passes on the coccygeal magnetic center of both Yogi and Yogini in order to help them to awaken their Kundalini.

A text of Yoga advises the Yogis to hold their respiration if they are in the danger of falling into orgasm. The text states, "If the disciple holds the respiration, his semen will not be spilled, even when he is embraced by the most tender and attractive of women."

Many magical positions exist in the east for the performance of the sexual act called Maithuna.

Female Yoginis must marvelously contract their vaginal muscles; this is how they avoid the orgasm and the ejaculation of their feminine sexual liquor. This is how their Kundalini awakens.

Tantric texts state that even when the semen is at the breaking point of being ejaculated, the Yogi must retain it at any cost, in other words, the semen must not be spilled.

The Yogi enters into ecstasy during the sexual act. Nirvana is attained with this type of sexual ecstasy. This is "to ride on the tiger;" this is how the Yogis consider this sexual act named Maithuna.

The sexual positions of Maithuna are numerous and they choose the one they wish. All of these sexual positions are found illustrated in the *Kama Kalpa,* a book of Sex Yoga. In one of them, the Yogi performs the Maithuna seated on the ground with his legs crossed in the oriental style; the Yogini sits on his legs and absorbs the phallus, thereafter she crosses her legs behind the Yogi's lower back in such a way that the Yogi is enveloped by her legs.

Sometimes the inverted embrace is utilized, within which, for very sacred and symbolic reasons, the Yogini executes the active part. The Yogi represents the apparently motionless spirit while she, the Yogini, represents nature in motion. Thus, in the supreme moment of the sexual act when the orgasm is approaching, the Yogini performs the more terrible and violent sexual contractions in order to avoid the spasm and the orgasmic ejaculation. The Yogis take advantage of this moment for the most frightful concentration and the most remarkable meditation. This is how they attain Illumination, Ecstasy, Samadhi.

Nevertheless, in the Western World, any matrimony can practice Maithuna without using these difficult positions from the east of the world. It is enough to pray to the Holy Spirit before the practice, asking for His assistance, and thereafter to perform the sexual act in the western style; the couple must withdraw before the orgasm. The semen must never be ejaculated in one's life.

The foolish scientists of Black Magic believe that this practice is dangerous and that can bring congestion to the prostate, urethra, and seminal vesicles. This concept of the foolish scientists is a solemn falsity. We, the Gnostics, practice this sexual act throughout our entire lives, and we have never suffered of problems with the prostate or the urethra or the seminal vesicles.

There is no doubt that matrimonies can reach supreme happiness with Maithuna.

This is how the joy of the honeymoon is perpetuated throughout the entire life. With this sexual act, there is true happiness; each time, the couple feels more the need for caresses and for performing the sexual act, without getting weary or tired of it. With this type of sexual act, divorces will end in the world. We enter into Nirvana with this type of sexual act.

Couples can pray and meditate back against back in the oriental style if they wish, thus begging, beseeching the Holy Spirit, to grant them the joy of receiving the Fire.

It is false to asseverate that Maithuna damages the prostate and produces prostatitis. All of us who practice Maithuna enjoy splendid health.

In the beginning, the Maithuna is sacrifice, yet after some time Maithuna is complete sexual satisfaction and supreme joy.

All of those theories that the foolish scientists render in order to combat Maithuna are absolutely false, and those who allow themselves to be cheated by the "reason without reason" of these tenebrous ones, will inevitably be transformed into inhabitants of the abyss.

We are initiating the New Aquarian Era and humanity will be divided in two bands: Those who accept White Tantrism, and those who will define themselves for the Black; in other words, those who will accept the ejaculation of their semen and those who will not accept it; those who will continue with the ejaculation of their semen, and those who will not continue with the ejaculation of it; White Tantric People and Black Tantric ones, that is all. Speaking in an occult manner we would say: White Magicians and Black Magicians. These are the two bands of the New Aquarian Era.

Frederick Nietzsche stated the following in his book *Thus Spoke Zarathustra:*

> Voluptuousness: to all hair-shirted despisers of the body,
> a sting and stake; and, cursed as "the world," by all the
> afterworldly: for it mocks and befools all erring, misinferring
> teachers.

> Voluptuousness: to the rabble, the slow fire at which it is
> burnt; to all wormy wood, to all stinking rags, the prepared
> heat and stew furnace.

> Voluptuousness: to free hearts, a thing innocent and free,
> the garden-happiness of the earth, all the future's thanks-
> overflow to the present.

> Voluptuousness: only to the withered a sweet poison; to the
> lion-willed, however, the great cordial, and the reverently
> saved wine of wines.

Voluptuousness: the great symbolic happiness of a higher happiness and highest hope. For to many is marriage promised, and more than marriage,-

-To many that are more unknown to each other than man and woman:- and who has fully understood how unknown to each other are man and woman!

Indeed, love is a terribly divine, cosmic phenomenon. When the man officiates at the altar of supreme sexual sacrifice, he can, in that moment, direct his entire voluptuousness towards all of his magnetic centers and make them vibrate, sparkle and shine. We are like remarkably divine Gods in those moments of supreme sexual voluptuousness.

The sacred scriptures state, "Ask and it shall be given onto you; knock and it shall be open onto you." Indeed, within the supreme moment of the sexual act is the precise moment in which we can ask the Third Logos (the Holy Spirit) for all of those longed-for powers. The tremendous power of the forces of Shiva, the Third Logos, transforms us into Gods.

Much is being said about meditation and ecstasy (Samadhi). Indeed, the best hour for meditation and ecstasy is the hour of sexual voluptuousness. The sexual forces produce the ecstasy. Through meditation, we must transform the voluptuousness into ecstasy.

During the sexual act and after the sexual act, when the voluptuousness is still vibrating, we pass through the *sacrificius intelectus*. Indeed only the creative emotion can takes to the ecstasy.

Only the one who is capable of crying when praying to the Third Logos before the sexual act and after the sexual act can enter into Nirvana; only the one who is capable of becoming inebriated with the voluptuousness without spilling the semen can be transformed into a remarkable, divine God.

Those who learn how to wisely enjoy the voluptuousness without spilling the semen are transformed into absolutely happy beings.

The Perfect Matrimony is the basis of the Path for the Social Christ. Unfortunately, in modern life, matrimony has transformed into a frivolity which is distant from wisdom. This is why marriages collapse; this is the cause of many divorces. It is necessary to study Gnosis, it is urgent to go back into the mystical celebrations of the mysteries of love. It is urgent to learn how to enjoy the delights of love. It is urgent to comprehend that with voluptuousness the Angel is born within our own selves. Only the Angels can enter into the kingdom.

White Tantrism has the science in order to end divorce and to preserve the honeymoon throughout one's entire life. The home is the foundation of a Christian society. White Tantrism with its famous Maithuna is the clue of divine sexual happiness.

Index

A

Abundance 21, 24
Abyss 37, 38, 40, 67, 68, 75
Accidents 16
Action 10, 19, 27, 32, 33, 46, 59, 60
Adi 14
Adulterer 35
Adulteries 28
Adultery 67, 68
Affection 60
Affirming 33
Ain Soph 52
Air 5, 14, 15, 16
Airplane accidents 16
Akash 14, 15, 17
Alcohol 28
Alcoholic larvae 39
Alcoholism 35, 39
American Yearbook 15
Amphora of Salvation 66, 67
Angel 77
Anger 4, 5, 56, 57, 70
Animals 50
Ant 28
Antipathy 55
Apas 14, 15, 16, 17
Appreciation 10
Aquarian Era 75
Architect 7
Argue 16
Ark 68
Arrogance 4
Artists 15
Asleep 39, 41, 47, 61
Aspiration 54
Astrological Yearbook 15
Atom 14, 58
Atomic atmosphere 38
Attention 4, 8, 55, 60, 61
Attraction 49
Audio-visual system 37
Aurora 14
Avocados 50

Awaken 67
Awakened 61, 65
Awakening 39, 61
Ayocosmos 52

B

Bandhas 73
Bee 28
Beheading 62
Being 21, 22, 28, 45
Beliefs 61
Benevolence 16
Bible 22, 29, 61
Binah 52
Bitterness 34, 35
Black bread 50
Black Magic 74
Black Magicians 75
Blame 3, 32
Blind 53
Bliss 49
Blood 49, 50
Body 4, 9, 21, 27, 28, 29, 33, 39, 40,
    41, 43, 46, 47, 49, 50, 53, 58,
    60, 61
Body of the Mind 58
Boxing 45
Brain 7, 8, 9, 11, 19, 28, 39, 59
Bread 50
Breathing 5
Brutality 61
Buddhism ii, 71
Bullfights 45
Business 9, 10, 14, 15, 16, 19, 20, 27,
    28, 29, 36, 49

C

Calm 31, 33
Cannibals 50
Capitalism 24
Carbonic acid 50
Cattle 50
Causal World 53

Cave 53
Cells 49
Centrifugal 46
Centrifuge 46
Centripetal 46
Cephas 67
Cerebrum 43
Change 8, 9, 24, 28, 50, 53, 56, 58
Chaos 54
Character 49
Charity 16
Chatter 57, 58
Chesed 52
Children 7, 37, 45
Chochmah 52
Christ 20, 52, 53, 66, 67, 68, 77
Christ-centrism 20
Christic principle 53
Christify 68
Circumstances 4, 8, 9, 10, 13
Cirrhosis 36
Clairvoyance 30, 61
Clairvoyant 54
Clairvoyants 27, 38
Classical Music 45
Clothing 23, 27
Coitus Reservatus 71
Comedies 55, 56
Comic books 45
Common good 20
Competition 25
Comprehension 20, 21, 24, 25, 27, 30,
    31, 33, 34, 37, 40, 41, 54, 58
Concentration v, vi, 8, 9, 11, 19, 20,
    22, 26, 34, 38, 40, 41, 62, 73, 74
Concepts 61
Conflict 6, 23, 28, 31, 32, 33, 34
Contradiction 6, 31, 32, 33, 34
Consciousness 25, 28, 53, 54, 60, 61,
    62
Contemplation 41
Contradiction 6, 31, 32, 33, 34
Corn flour 50
Corpse posture 9
Cosmic Justice 10
Cosmic Mind 7, 8, 43
Cosmic Soul 46
Cosmos 41, 43, 58

Courtesy 27
Covetousness 25, 26, 27, 28, 44
Cow milk 50
Creation 57
Criminals 3
Criticism 3, 10
Critique Of Pure Reason 43
Crucified 67
Cruelty 61
Crystallization 9, 10, 13, 56

D
Darkness 43, 53, 54
Dawn 14
Death 15, 30, 35, 36, 37, 53, 66, 67, 68
Defects 21, 22, 40, 62
Delirium tremens 38
Demons 38
Denying 33
Desire 1, 10, 19, 21, 28, 33, 34, 53,
    57, 61
Desires 19, 21, 28, 33, 34, 66
Despise 10
Destruction 54
Detachment 25
Deuterocosmos 52
Devil 27, 28
Devotion 11
Dialogues 57
Dianoia 61
Digestive system 36
Directed attention 55
Discord 31
Disillusionments 21
Disintegration 21, 39, 57, 58, 62
Distrust 21
Divine Mother 62
Divorce 35, 65, 66, 68, 69, 77
DO 52
Dream 60, 65
Dreamer 60, 61
Dreams 60, 61
Dress 27
Drowsiness 41
Drunkard 35, 36, 37, 38
Dry laws 37
Dungeon 53, 54

E

Ear drum 39
Earth 7, 14, 23, 43
Ecstasy 14, 38, 41, 70, 71, 73, 74, 76
Eggs 50
Ego 21, 39, 40, 60, 67
Egotism 4, 20
Eikasia 61
Ejaculation 71, 73, 74, 75
Elephant 50
Eliminate 22, 35, 49, 50, 56, 57, 58, 62
Elimination 56, 58, 59, 60
Emotion 40, 55
Emotional 62
Emotions 55
Employee 4, 28, 33
Emptiness 25
Encourage 10
Encouragement 10
Energy 8, 10, 11, 13, 14, 29, 58
Enthusiasm 10
Envy 21, 44
Errors 3, 20, 40, 58
Essence 53, 54, 58
Eternal 53
Ether 13, 14
Evasions 59
Evil 14, 23, 27, 28, 45
Excessive work 4
Excitement 4
Explaining 33, 37
External world 57
Extremes 56

F

FA 52
Failure 13, 21
Faith 11
Fame 23
Fanaticism 21, 61
Fantasy 56
Fatigue 4
Fear 21
Ferocity 50
Fire 14, 16, 17, 65-77
Fisher of men 19
Five-pointed Star 39

Five centers 60
Flattery 10
Flour 50
Food 10, 23, 27, 36, 49, 50
Fornicate 56, 65
Fornication 28, 29, 68
Fornicator 35
Fornicators 67
Four levels of men 60
Four States of Consciousness 60, 61
Fourth dimension 38, 39
Franklin, Benjamin 22
Freedom 33, 54
Freud 10

G

Galaxy 52
Galvan's Calendar 15
Gastric ulcers 5
Geburah 52
Genesis 53
Geniuses 29
Glands 49
Gluttony 44
Gnosis 1, 2, 77
Gnostic doctor 50
God 10, 21, 22, 38, 40, 44
Gods 38, 41
Goethe 53
Good 1, 10, 11, 14, 15, 16, 17, 20, 23,
    27, 28, 31, 37, 38, 44, 45, 49,
    54, 61
Gospels 22
Gossip 32
Grave 33
Great Arcanum 67
Great Reality 25, 45, 46
Guardian of the Threshold 29
Guns 45
Guru 73

H

Happiness 19, 21, 23, 24, 29, 49, 68,
    70, 74, 76, 77
Happy 3, 8, 16, 20, 24, 28
Hate 3
Hatred 21, 25, 44

Health 7, 8, 16, 49
Heart 9, 40, 59, 60, 65, 66, 67, 68
Hell 38
Heresy 46
Hermetic Work 56
Herrera, Dr. Olaya 27
Hinduism 71
Hod 52
Holland 53
Holy Spirit 65, 69, 71, 74, 75, 76
Home 3, 27, 31, 37, 38
Honeymoon 74, 77
Horse 50
Human machine 60
Human Soul 53
Humiliate 10
Hungry 27
Hypocrisy 28

I
"I" 11, 20, 21, 25, 27, 28, 30, 40, 56,
      57, 58, 59, 60, 61, 62, 65, 66,
      67, 68, 70
Identification 31, 57
Idiots 29
Illumination 54, 74
Imagination 30, 39, 40, 44, 45, 46, 47
Immanuel Kant 43
Immoral 37
Impatience 4
Importance 7
India 70
Individual 10, 24, 25, 32, 42, 44, 46
Inferior emotions 55
Inferior Worlds 52
Infernos 38
Infinite 52
Infrasexual 66
Initiation 35, 37
Initiations 67
Inner Chatter 57, 58
Inner dialogues 57
Inner extremes 56
Inner Self 21, 40, 60, 62
Inner Silence 58
Inner worlds 57
Instinct 60

Instinctive 59
Intellect 59
Intellectual 1, 16, 56, 59, 60, 62
Intellectual center 56, 59
Intellectual works 16
Intelligence 9
Intelligent action 33
Internal Master 40
Internal silence 58
Internal state 49
Internal vision 26
Intoxication 35, 36, 37, 38
Intuition 33, 61

J
Jealousy 21, 70
Jesus 19, 67, 68, 72
Job 28, 33
John 67, 68
Judas 67, 68, 70
Judgement 58, 59
Jupiter 17
Justifications 59
Justify 3, 21, 25, 60

K
Kama Kalpa 74
Karma 10
Kether 52
Klipoth 52
Know 2
Knowledge 1, 2, 34, 54, 55
Krumm Heller, Dr. Arnold 50
Kundalini 65, 66, 67, 71, 73

L
La 52, 53
Larvae 38
Lasciviousness 60
Law of Karma 10
Law of Seven 52
Law of Universal Vibration 13
Laziness 44
Leave 9, 28, 47, 49
Lewdness 60, 65
Liberate 54
Lies 32

Life iv, 3, 7, 8, 10, 11, 13, 14, 16, 17,
   19, 20, 21, 27, 29, 31, 32, 33,
   37, 39, 55, 58
Light 13, 14, 30, 43, 53, 54, 57, 58, 62
Liver 36, 49
Lodge, Sir Oliver 13
Lost 54
Lottery tickets 16
Love 7, 8, 14, 15, 16, 21, 28, 40, 44, 45,
   49, 57, 60, 64, 65, 66, 67, 68,
   69, 70, 76, 77
Luck 13
Lust 44, 56, 60
Lying 16

M

Machine 49, 60
Macrocosmos 52
Magazines 45
Magnet 49
Magnetic field 13
Maithuna 73, 74, 75, 77
Malkuth 52
Manhood 35
Marriage 16
Mars 17
Materialization 10
Material things 24, 25
Matrimony 65, 67, 70, 74, 77
Matter 13
Mayan Initiates 73
Meat 49, 50
Meditate 10, 38, 40, 73, 75
Meditation vi, 10, 14, 15, 26, 38, 40,
   41, 46, 55, 58, 62, 73, 74, 76
Memories 56
Memory 21, 28, 40
Mental anguish 33
Mental Body 43, 44, 58
Mental calm 31
Mental conflict 33, 34
Mental energy 8
Mental epidemics 44
Mental force 7, 9
Mental hygiene 45
Mental power 8, 10, 11, 19, 39, 46
Mental projections 8

Mental silence 33, 58
Mental waves 7, 8, 11, 20, 28, 29, 44
Merchandise 16
Mercury 17
Mesocosmos 52
Mi 52, 53
Michelangelo 45
Microcosmos 52
Milk 50
Milky Way 53
Mind iv, 1, 7, 8, 9, 10, 11, 19, 20, 21,
   23, 24, 25, 28, 29, 31, 33, 34,
   38, 40, 41, 42, 43, 44, 45, 46,
   47, 58, 59, 60, 62, 65, 68
Mirror 29
Misery 13, 14, 21, 25
Misfortune 13
Missiles 13
Molecular World 60
Money 7, 8, 13, 14, 16, 20, 23, 24, 25,
   69, 70
Moon 17
Moral tragedy 35
Morelos 54
Moses 53
Motion 15
Motor-instinctive-sexual 62
Motor center 59
Mouth 5
Movie theatres 45
Mudras 73
Music 31
Mysteries of Nature 38

N

Napoleon 54
Nature 61
Necessity 25, 26, 27, 36, 37, 54, 56, 61
Needle 11
Negative state 55
Negative thought 55, 57, 62
Nervous 5
Nervous system 4
Netzach 52
Neurasthenia 4, 15
Nietzsche 75
Nirvana 71, 73, 74, 75, 76

Non-Directed attention 55
Nose 5
Not thinking 33
Nourishment 7
Nous 61
Nutrition 49, 50

O
Observation 55, 56, 57, 58, 59, 62
Observe 30, 34, 50, 54, 55, 56, 57, 60
Obstinacy 34
Octave 52
Om 11
Operas 45
Opinions 61
Optimism 49
Orgasm 71, 73, 74
Osmotherapy 39

P
Pain 25, 32
Passion 28, 61, 65, 66, 68, 69, 70, 71
Passions 28, 67, 70
Patience 4, 62
Peace 5, 6, 11, 17, 21, 22, 24, 30, 31,
    32, 33, 34, 41, 44, 47, 50
Perfection 21, 24
Perfect Matrimony 68, 70, 77
Perfumes 39
Personality 9
Peter 67, 68
Philosophical Stone 67
Photomentometer 7
Physical body 9, 33, 39, 40, 41, 46, 47,
    49, 52, 53, 60
Physical needs 23, 25, 26
Physical world 8, 53, 57
Pineal Gland 28, 29, 30
Pistis 61
Planet 52
Plantains 50
Plenitude 21, 54
Point of view 19, 20, 49
Poison 44, 50, 65, 71, 76
Police 45
Political party 24
Pornographic magazines 45

Posture 9
Poverty 21, 24
Power 7, 8, 10, 11, 19, 21, 23, 29, 30,
    39, 46, 49
Powers 53, 66, 71, 76
Prana 14
Pranayamas 73
Pratyahara 73
Pray 15, 29, 40, 41, 61, 74, 75
Prayer 11, 29, 30, 40, 60, 61, 62
Prestige 23
Pride 3, 4, 44
Prithvi 14, 15, 16, 17
Problems 11, 19, 28, 31, 32, 33, 34,
    42, 44, 53
Progress 3, 28
Project 8
Projections 8
Projects 13
Prosperous 11
Prostate 74, 75
Prostatitis 75
Prostitution 65, 69
Protein 50
Protests 56
Protocosmos 52
Psyche 56, 62
Psychological dependence 25
Psychological errors 58
Psychologist 10, 55
Psychology 49
Purchase 16
Putrefaction 50

Q
Quarrels 16
Quiet 57
Quietude 58

R
Radiation 13
Radio 13, 58
Radioactive 19
Rage 57
Ray of Cosmic Justice 10
Ray of Creation 52
RE 52

Reaction 3, 33, 46, 57
Reality 53
Reasons 59
Rebels without a cause 45
Relaxation 9, 20, 39, 40
Resentment 3, 70
Resistance 3, 46
Respiration 73
Rest 4, 17, 25
Retreat 31
Ridiculousness 56, 57
Rose 39

S
Sacrifice 71, 75, 76
Sacrificius intelectus 76
Samadhi 14, 38, 61, 70, 71, 73, 74, 76
Satan 21, 28, 29, 30
Satisfaction 7, 23, 24, 33
Saturn 17
Scientists 1, 13, 74, 75
Second Death 68
Self-confidence 47
Self-criticism 70
Self-observation 56, 57, 58, 61, 62
Self-remembering 60, 61, 62
Semen 71, 73, 74, 75, 77
Seminal vesicles 74
Sensation 24
Sense 56
Sensitive 60
Separability 46
Seseras, Jose M. 13
Seven 52
Seven Churches 66
Seven Tattwas 14
Sex 56, 60, 66, 67, 68, 70, 71
Sexual act 70, 71, 73, 74, 75, 76
Sexual center 59, 60
Sexual energies 29
Sexual impulse 10
Sexual intercourse 73
Sexual organs 29
Sexual satisfaction 7, 75
Sexual union 71
Sex Yoga 71, 73, 74
Shakti 73

Shelter 23, 27
Shiva 73, 76
Si 52
Silence 33, 34, 40, 58
Silence of the mind 33, 34
Silent 57
Silk thread 11
Sin 33
Sincere 3, 10
Sincerity 19, 27, 29
Six rays 54
Sixth Commandment 29
Sixth sense 30
Sleep 7, 22, 26, 28, 30, 41, 47, 61
Sleeping 39, 60
Smile 27, 28, 29
Smoker 35
Social Christ 77
Social position 23
Social prestige 23
Social status 70
Social system 24
Society 32, 37, 53
Sol 52, 53
Solar Plexus 28, 29
Solar System 52
Solution 31, 32, 57
Soul vi, 27, 28, 29, 30, 41, 43, 46, 47,
    53, 54, 57, 65, 66, 67
Soybeans 50
Speak 57
Spirit 4, 13, 21, 41, 46
Spiritual Sun 52
Splendor 13
Star 26, 39
Star of six rays 54
State 49, 55, 60, 61, 62
Stealing 16
Stomach 36
Stupidities 57
Subconsciousness 39
Subjective elements 53
Subterfuges 59
Success 3, 7, 8, 9, 10, 13, 16, 19, 20,
    22, 28, 29, 44
Suffering 25, 35, 60
Suicides 16

Sulphur 39
Sun 17, 43, 52, 53, 66, 70
Sunrise 17
Sympathy 49

T
Tantra 71
Tantrism 63, 65, 67, 69, 71, 73, 75, 77
Tattwas 13, 14, 15, 17
Tattwic Timetable 15
Techniques 54
Tejas 14, 15, 16, 17
Telementometer 7
Telepathy 28
Television 13
Theories 61
Theosophists 43
Thinking 26, 56
Third Eye 17
Third Logos 76
Third State 62
Thought 4, 8, 9, 10, 19, 28, 29, 30, 38,
        40, 43, 44, 45, 55, 56, 57, 58,
        60, 62
Three Brains 62
Tiphereth 52
Tragedy 57
Tranquility 31
Transformation 56
Treatment 39
Tritocosmos 52
Truth 19, 24

U
Ulcer 5, 36
Unconsciousness 61
United States 22
Universal Mind 7, 42, 43, 44, 45, 46
Universe 7, 10, 13, 43, 44, 45
Urethra 74

V
Vanity 3, 4, 23, 34
Vayu 14, 15, 16, 17
Vedas 70
Vegetables 49, 50
Vegetarian Diet 49

Velocity 15
Vengeance 10
Venus 17
Verb 11
Vibration 13, 14, 15
Vices 28
Victory 8
Violence 21, 32
Virility 66
Virtue 22, 37, 53
Vision 26
Vitamins 50
Voluptuousness 76, 77

W
Wants 21
War 25, 28
Water 8, 14, 16, 49, 56
We 11, 20
Wedding Garment 66
Wheat 50
White bread 50
White Magicians 75
Will 44, 47
Willpower 47
Wireless system 28
Wisdom 33, 45
Word 67, 68
Work 4, 11, 29, 56, 60, 62
World 4, 8, 10, 24, 25, 27, 29, 43, 53,
        55, 57, 61
World of the Mind 8
Worry 33, 40
Wrestling 45

Y
Yoga 71, 73, 74
Yogas 71

Books by the Same Author

Aquarian Message,
Aztec Christic Magic
Book of the Dead
Book of the Virgin of Carmen
Buddha's Necklace
Christ Will
Christmas Messages (various)
Cosmic Ships
Cosmic Teachings of a Lama
Didactic Self-Knowledge
Dream Yoga (collected writings)
Elimination of Satan's Tail
Esoteric Course of Runic Magic
Esoteric Treatise of Hermetic Astrology
Esoteric Treatise of Theurgy
Fundamental Education
Fundamental Notions of Endocrinology
Gnostic Anthropology
Gnostic Catechism
The Great Rebellion
Greater Mysteries
Igneous Rose
The Initiatic Path in the Arcana of Tarot
    and Kabbalah

Introduction to Gnosis
Kabbalah of the Mayan Mysteries
Lamasery Exercises
Logos Mantra Theurgy
Manual of Practical Magic
Mysteries of Fire: Kundalini Yoga
Mystery of the Golden Blossom
Occult Medicine & Practical Magic
Parsifal Unveiled
The Perfect Matrimony
Pistis Sophia Unveiled
Revolution of Beelzebub
Revolution of the Dialectic
Revolutionary Psychology
Secret Doctrine of Anahuac
Three Mountains
Transmutation of Sexual Energy
Treatise of Sexual Alchemy
Yellow Book
Yes, There is Hell, a Devil, and Karma
Zodiacal Course
150 Answers from Master Samael Aun Weor

To learn more about Gnosis, visit gnosticteachings.org.

Thelema Press is a non-profit publisher dedicated to spreading the sacred universal doctrine to suffering humanity. All of our works are made possible by the kindness and generosity of sponsors. If you would like to make a tax-deductible donation, you may send it to the address below, or visit our website for other alternatives. If you would like to sponsor the publication of a book, please contact us at 212-501-6106 or help@gnosticteachings.org.

Thelema Press
PMB 192, 18645 SW Farmington Rd., Aloha OR 97007 USA
Phone: 212-501-6106 · Fax: 212-501-1676

Visit us online at:
gnosticteachings.org
gnosticradio.org
gnosticschool.org
gnosticstore.org
gnosticvideos.org